THE TITMICE OF THE
BRITISH ISLES

JOHN A. G. BARNES

DAVID & CHARLES
NEWTON ABBOT   LONDON
NORTH POMFRET (VT)   VANCOUVER

ISBN 0 7153 6955 5
Library of Congress Catalog Card Number 74-33156

Set in 11 on 13pt Bembo
and printed in Great Britain
by Latimer Trend & Company Limited Plymouth
for David & Charles (Holdings) Limited
South Devon House Newton Abbot Devon

Published in the United States of America
by David & Charles Inc
North Pomfret Vermont 05053 USA

Published in Canada
by Douglas David & Charles Limited
132 Philip Avenue North Vancouver BC

Contents

List of Illustrations

———◆———

Preface

The titmice are probably the best-loved and most closely observed group of birds in Britain today. In acrobatic agility they have few rivals, and their plumage, even when it lacks brilliance of colour, has an attractive clear-cut neatness. The facial markings of the blue tit in particular give it an expression of perky alertness and intelligence, and its persistent curiosity and constant activity make it a most entertaining bird to watch. If words like 'personality' and 'character' may ever be used in describing a wild bird they are surely more applicable to blue tits and great tits than to any other common species. In addition to more endearing qualities they often display a self-confident, aggressive or irritable manner that invites human comparisons, and many of them show marked individuality in their breeding habits and feeding methods. The fascination of watching tits owes much to these differences in temperament and manner between species and individuals and to the adaptability of their behaviour.

Moreover the common tit species are becoming increasingly familiar garden birds both in town and country, and with patience they can be persuaded to feed from the hand. Indeed blue tits may be so fearless and inquisitive in autumn that they make their way into occupied houses in spite of determined efforts to exclude them. Great and blue tits often seem to prefer even the crudest box to a natural hole for nest-building, and in the absence of nest-boxes will use other man-made sites such as letter-boxes, inverted plant-pots and hollow posts of gates and fences. This association with man and his domestic environment makes the tits particularly well suited for study by people

9

with limited leisure. Because of their attractive characteristics tits are now actively encouraged to feed and breed in thousands of British gardens, and their occasional misdemeanours with fruit, milk bottles and wall-paper are usually treated with generous tolerance. In fact their bold impudence seems to have a charm of its own.

The only serious rival to the tits in popular appeal is the robin, acclaimed in public opinion polls as 'Bird of Britain'. With its confiding tameness, sweet and slightly melancholy song and blameless diet it has a safe place in the affections of bird-lovers; but in recent years the blue tit has been a very close competitor as a model for Christmas cards and calendars. Certainly the annual expenditure of money on food, feeding appliances and nest-boxes intended only for tits has grown at a phenomenal rate.

Yet this affection for the tits is a comparatively recent development. In 1837 Yarrell wrote in his *History of British Birds* that the blue tit's 'beauty and sprightliness are not so highly appreciated as they deserve', and 'there are few birds which are commonly believed to do more harm than this, and by nearly all gardeners it is regarded as one of their worst foes'. Perhaps this change in popular attitudes is a reflection of social conditions. The vogue of the nightingale, beloved of poets from Aristophanes to Eliot, has probably always been chiefly a literary one, and it could only be widespread in a rural community. The rise of the robin in popular favour belongs to a period of private gardens in town and country, and the recent cult of the tit family may be the product of a comparatively prosperous and leisured society in which wild birds are regarded as intrinsic assets to a garden and not just as allies or enemies in the business of food production.

In the last thirty years the tit family has achieved another kind of popularity, as a subject for scientific inquiry. Of all European passerine species the great tit is perhaps the most suitable for detailed study in the wild. It is found, often abundantly, in woodlands throughout the continent, and the wide variations in the number of eggs laid and young reared by different individuals and in different conditions make it a specially useful subject for the investigation of population problems in birds. Its strong preference for nest-boxes is a valuable asset in studies of its breeding biology. In winter the mixed tit flocks are easily heard and seen, and as the British tits are not migratory their local movements and ecological preferences can be conveniently studied in a limited area. Furthermore, the birds can usually be trapped without much difficulty and individually ringed. Consequently more intensive studies have been made of the tit species than of any other group of small birds, and further research goes on.

There is in fact such a wealth of information available about the titmice, mainly in scientific periodicals, that it would be difficult to summarise it even in bare outline in a single volume. This book gives a general introduction to this group of birds and then discusses in greater detail certain especially interesting aspects of their lives. Even so the writing of each chapter has provided a taxing exercise in selection and compression. Personal observations have been included partly to provide comparisons from other parts of Britain with the published data from certain intensively studied woods in the south and east of England, and partly in the belief that first-hand accounts are often more readable than second-hand summaries. Perhaps also readers may be encouraged to record their own observations about the tits and other common birds. Even if such observations are of limited scientific value they will provide a great deal of interest and enjoyment for those who make them, and surely no further justification is required. The following chapters should dispel any idea that all questions have been answered about even the commonest and most thoroughly investigated of our native birds.

1 The Tit Family

In 1950 the question of what is and what is not a British tit would have seemed simple to answer. The family Paridae, the titmice, included six species of the genus *Parus* which breed regularly in at least some parts of the British Isles: the great tit *Parus major*, blue tit *P. caeruleus*, coal tit *P. ater*, crested tit *P. cristatus*, and the closely similar marsh and willow tits *P. palustris* and *P. montanus*. (The accepted scientific name for the willow tit in 1950 was *Parus atricapillus*, but since then the European and Asiatic willow tit has been recognised as a different species from the black-capped chickadee *P. atricapillus* of North America.) Two other birds belonging to different genera, the long-tailed tit *Aegithalos caudatus* and the bearded tit *Panurus biarmicus*, were included in the tit family, both by virtue of their English names and by the general agreement of the great majority of taxonomists. No other member of the Paridae had been recorded in the British Isles.

By 1970 the situation was different. As long ago as 1937, in the *Checklist of Birds of the World* (J. L. Peters), the bearded tit was placed in the family of Muscicapidae, which includes warblers, flycatchers, chats and thrushes. A similar classification has been adopted by most modern authorities. In *The Birds of the Palearctic Fauna*, 1959, Charles Vaurie places the bearded tit in a sub-family Timaliinae of the family Muscicapidae, and he also assigns the long-tailed tit to a separate family, the Aegithalidae, of which it is the only European representative.

One does not need to be an expert taxonomist to notice several untitlike characteristics in the bearded tit. It differs from the *Parus* species in its specialised reed-bed habitat, its courtship behaviour, its open nest, the colouration of the eggs, the pattern of white spots on the nestling's palate, the occasional habit of walking and running on the ground, and the fact that the sexes are markedly different in plumage. The long-tailed tit resembles the other tits more closely in appearance, habitat and habits and often associates with them in mixed flocks. It differs in its very short wings and very long tail, and most of all in the type of nest it makes. It does not nest in a hole like the *Parus* species, but builds a beautiful oval domed structure of moss, lichen and feathers in a bush or hedge or in the fork of a tree.

A single individual of another European species, the penduline tit *Remiz pendulinus*, was observed at Spurn, Yorkshire, on 22 and 28 October 1966, the first record for the British Isles. Its normal breeding range in Europe was, until recently, restricted to the east and south, where it is found, chiefly, though not exclusively, in marshy localities or in dense vegetation on the banks of water courses. But since about 1950 there has been a marked expansion northwards and westwards: nests have been found in Denmark and birds seen in Finland, north-west Germany, Holland, Belgium, northern France and the Channel Islands. Although the penduline tit shows some titlike characteristics of appearance and behaviour it differs from the *Parus* species in its pale head and black mask, and in the jerky lateral movement of the tail. Its nest is unlike that of any other European species; the structure, made of grasses and vegetable down, is shaped rather like a chemist's retort, with a short tubular entrance at the side. Vaurie also places this bird in a separate family, the Remizidae.

Regretfully, the bearded tit, beautiful and fascinating as it is, is excluded from further discussion in this book, both on grounds of classification and because it is so different from the typical tits in habitat and behaviour. The penduline tit will also be omitted. Its membership of the tit family is doubtful, and also, in spite of its recent expansion of range in Europe, it can only be regarded as a very rare vagrant to the British Isles. On the other hand the long-tailed tit is so often seen in the company of other tits, and in many respects resembles them so closely, that there will be frequent references to it, even though the main emphasis will be on the six British representatives of the genus *Parus*.

According to the latest classification there are 45 species of tits, the genus *Parus*, in the world. Ten of these are found in North America,

10 in Africa south of the Sahara, 9 in Europe and 23 in Asia (including 7 of the European species).

The British bird-watcher abroad, meeting one of these species for the first time, will have little difficulty in recognising it as belonging to the titmouse family. There is something about their build, markings, movements and habits that is characteristic and unmistakable. Always they are small, none of them as big as a house sparrow, short-necked and compact in body, with rounded wings. Their bills are short and strong, their legs and feet sturdy, and their gymnastic activity on twig or food basket is a delight to watch. Although the colour pattern of the plumage varies in detail from one species to another, certain features are constant in nearly all the European species: they have white cheeks and dark, often black caps, with the sole exception of the azure tit *Parus cyanus* which has a conspicuously white crown. The wings and back are some shade of grey-brown, greenish or blue and the underparts whitish or yellow. The general effect is neat and clear-cut: the body plumage is not streaked or spotted even in juvenile birds. The sexes are closely similar in appearance—in most species they cannot be reliably distinguished in the field.

It is not so easy to make valid generalisations about the 'song' or vocal characteristics of the genus, but nevertheless a certain tit quality is often noticeable in their utterances. Although each species has its individual vocabulary many of their calls have a nasal or metallic timbre, and the song usually consists of the repetition of a simple phrase of one, two or three syllables. The variety of vocal expression achieved within this framework, especially by the great tit, is remarkable.

The tits generally frequent trees, but the more adaptable species find open country with scattered bushes or hedgerows an acceptable habitat, and the blue tit is commonly found in extensive reed-beds. The habitat preferences of the different species are discussed in Chapters 3 and 7.

Their food is varied, including both animal and vegetable matter. In the smaller species much of it consists of particles so minute that they cannot be identified by the field observer even at close quarters and with the best of optical aids. Several of the northern species regularly hide seeds and other food items in excess of their immediate needs, a habit that they share with the related nuthatch. This behaviour is most commonly seen in late summer and autumn but may in fact be practised at any time of year. It is discussed in more detail in Chapter 7.

Although the movements of tits through the trees in their natural woodland habitat are direct and purposeful, the flight of the smaller species over longer distances looks jerky and laboured, with irregular dips and rises. A blue tit crossing a wide open space—which it is often reluctant to do—is curiously reminiscent of a child learning to swim and struggling to keep his head above water. Great tits are stronger on the wing, but even they show nothing like the buoyant, bounding flight of many of the finches or the long smooth undulations of the wagtails. So it is not surprising to find that in general tits are not migratory, and in the greater part of their European range most individuals probably never travel more than two or three miles from their birthplace. However, there is evidence of regular southward and westward migration of great tits from the far north and east of Europe, dispersal movements of a proportion of juveniles and, in some years, large-scale irruptions into western Europe, which may also involve blue tits and sometimes coal tits. These movements will be discussed further in Chapter 6.

The tits in general are at least partly gregarious, outside the breeding season, and move about over a limited area in mixed flocks, which often include goldcrests, one or two nuthatches and treecreepers and, in late summer and autumn, warblers. But some pairs or individuals even of the most social species may remain detached and sedentary throughout the year.

Certain features of breeding behaviour are also common to all the genus *Parus*. They all normally nest in holes, some species usually selecting holes in trees, sometimes excavated by themselves, others preferring to build in cavities in the ground or in masonry. All have eggs with whitish ground-colour spotted with red. The clutch is usually larger than in the case of passerine species with open nests, and the fledging period longer. Nestlings in open nests are more vulnerable than those in holes, so early dispersal has survival value for the former, while the longer period in the safety of a hole gives young tits more time to develop their powers of flight.

In addition to the family characteristics of structure, plumage, habit and voice, the *Parus* tits have in common certain traits of disposition or character. They are excitable, irascible little birds with a temperament and a temper fitted to their quick movements and expressive calls. Their swift reactions of anger or irritation are not directed only against members of their own species or genus but also against much larger birds and interfering mammals, including cats, dogs, squirrels and humans. Anyone who wishes to handle titmice for ringing, weighing or measuring, or to inspect the contents of nest-boxes, must be prepared to be pecked, bitten, hissed at and subjected to outbursts of Paridine vituperation.

It is not surprising that generally sedentary species with a wide breeding range should develop local variations in colour and even in structure, and this has happened in the case of all the *Parus* species that occur in western Europe. When these differences are sufficiently definite and constant a geographical race, or subspecies, is designated with a trinomial scientific name. Thus the great tit which breeds in continental Europe is known as *Parus major major* and the British race as *P. major newtoni*. Many of the distinguishing characters of these races can only be detected by close examination and comparison of a number of skins, and expert taxonomists not infrequently disagree about the validity of some subspecies. Their task is complicated by the range of individual differences in plumage of some of the tits, even in a resident local population. The shade of the underparts is particularly variable in great and blue tits, ranging from brilliant canary yellow to a creamy off-white. Coal tits vary widely in the colouring of the flanks, which are greyish in some birds, buff or gingery in others. Observers should notice, however, that the blackish underparts sometimes shown by blue and coal tits are not a genuine colour variation, but are due to the wearing away of the tips of the contour feathers. Marsh tits generally run more true to type, but a few individuals show pale secondary wing feathers like those of the willow tit. In the following pages, the subspecies mentioned are those which have occurred, or might be expected, in the British Isles and which are recognised by Vaurie in *The Birds of the Palearctic Fauna*.

2 The British Tits

The descriptions of the British tit species in this chapter are largely concerned with identification, and so tend to emphasise the differences between them. However, most generalisations have exceptions, and the words 'always' and 'never' can seldom be safely used in distinguishing one species of tit from another by its habits. For example, all the British tits may sometimes be found breeding in coniferous woodland, but only the crested and coal tits show a preference for this habitat and the marsh tit is definitely rare in it. All the British tits have been recorded storing food, but the habit is very rare among blue and great tits and common among the others. There are similar gradations in food preferences and in flocking and migratory behaviour. This lack of rigid, invariable distinctions between the species is an indication of their close relationship.

Identification by sound, which is so important in studying woodland birds, raises the thorny problem of the representation of songs or calls on paper. B. W. Tucker's transcriptions in *The Handbook of British Birds* are among the best verbal representations I know, but who would recognise the great tit's scolding churr from the *Handbook* version: *chich-ich-ich-ich-ich* . . . ? Because of this difficulty only a few of the most commonly used and characteristic calls of each species are described here. Fortunately there are now available several excellent recordings of the songs and calls of the British tits, among other birds, and these can be a most valuable aid in the recognition of the different species, second only to actual observation in the field.

The sound spectrograph, an instrument which analyses sounds and can produce on paper a pattern representing the pitch, loudness and duration of the notes of a bird's song, can also be extremely useful to the ornithologist. A sound spectrogram is a visible, permanent and objective record, and it is especially helpful in the comparison of the songs of individual birds and in the detection of regional variations within a species. Even for the inexpert amateur it can give a general impression of the character of a bird's song, but for identification purposes he will find it inadequate without experience of the actual sounds from the bird itself or from a tape, radio or gramophone recording. This is especially true of a bird's call and alarm notes as distinct from its song. The technique of visual representation of bird vocalisation is steadily being developed and improved.

The **GREAT TIT**, *Parus major*, is so much bigger and more robust than the other British tits that mistaken identification might seem impossible. Its average length from bill-tip to end of tail is 5½ inches (14cm) compared with a maximum of about 4½ inches (11·5cm) for the other British species, and the wing, leg and bill measurements are correspondingly larger. Its build and movements give an impression of sturdy strength. But size alone is not always an easy criterion to apply, for example when a party of tits is moving through trees in full leaf. The great tit resembles the coal tit in its head pattern, with glossy black crown and throat and white cheeks, but it has only a small yellowish patch on the nape, where the coal tit has a conspicuous broad white stripe.

The most obvious distinguishing feature of the great tit is the broad black band down the centre of its yellow underparts: no other tit has comparable markings. A further distinction from the coal tit is in the wing pattern: the great tit has a single whitish bar across the wing, the coal tit a double one. The great tit's rather long tail with white on the outer feathers also differentiates it from the coal tit, which has a short tail without a white border.

The great tit is the only British tit in which the sexes can be distinguished in the field with reasonable certainty by plumage differences. The female not only shows less gloss on the black parts than the adult male, but the black band down the centre of the underparts is narrower and does not extend outwards to the legs. The male is sometimes noticeably bigger than the female. Juvenile birds, before their moult in August and September, have paler, softer colours, yellowish cheeks and dusty-looking, sooty caps and central bands. A first-winter bird in the hand can be distinguished from an older one by the fact that the fringes to the primary wing coverts are duller than those of the greater coverts, and the centre feather of the bastard wing is edged with green instead of bluish or grey.

The great tit is a highly vocal bird, and in natural surroundings is more often heard than seen. Its song and calls are louder than the other tits' and carry well. The song consists of the repetition of a phrase of two, three, or occasionally four syllables. One of the commonest forms may be represented as *tee-cher*, *tee-cher*, usually repeated from three to eight times. In some bird books this is referred to as 'saw-sharpening', but as many more people must have heard great tits singing than have ever heard saws being sharpened the comparison is not a very helpful one. Some males show a preference for one particular form of song, others change frequently from one pattern to another. An experienced male has a repertoire of four or five songs, or even more.

Apart from variations in its song the great tit has a very wide range of calls, some distinctive, others not unlike those of other tits. The late Miss Terry Gompertz, who made a detailed study of the songs and vocabulary of the great tit, distinguished forty different utterances from a single bird.[1] This individual constantly extended his vocabulary by 'adoption from his neighbours and by personal improvisation'. This apparent imitation may account for local variations or 'dialects'. Most bird-watchers will admit to having been puzzled at some time by an unfamiliar call in the woods, only to find that the mystery bird was a great tit. Two of its most frequent and characteristic calls are a metallic *tink*, repeated several times and resembling the note of a chaffinch, and a harsh scolding *churr*. The corresponding *churr* of the blue tit is quieter and less aggressive and the component notes are less distinct.

Another sound, though not a vocal one, often reveals the presence of a great tit: the loud hammering as the bird splits a hard seed or nut on a branch. This is a very familiar sound in winter in woods where yew seeds are available. The marsh tit also hammers open yew seeds, but its blows are more rapid and less resonant.

Few passerine species have a wider distribution in Eurasia than the great tit. Its breeding range extends from the British Isles to Japan, north to the arctic circle and south to north Africa, Iran, Ceylon and Indonesia. In the British Isles it is absent as a breeding bird from Orkney and Shetland, but great tits of continental origin appear there as passage migrants or even as winter residents. It is still very scarce and local in the Outer Hebrides but has become well established in the Isles of Scilly since about 1920. It is also during the present century that its breeding range has reached the extreme north of the Scottish mainland. Continental migrants reach Britain in varying numbers, occasionally in large irruptions.

The continental race of the great tit, *P. m. major*, extends from Scandinavia to Spain, Italy and the Balkans. Migrant birds of this race have frequently occurred in Britain, chiefly in the east and south. *P. m. newtoni*, the British subspecies, has a larger, thicker and wider bill and tends to be rather darker and greener on the mantle, but the differences cannot be reliably distinguished in the field.

The great tit is catholic in its habitat requirements. Although it is primarily a woodland species with a preference for deciduous trees, it is also found at all seasons in open country with bushes or hedges. It breeds readily among conifers, especially if nest-boxes are provided, but tends to desert such plantations in winter. It has adapted itself to urban conditions and this association with man is not simply the product of Anglo-Saxon ornithophily, as seems to be the case with the robin: great tits can be seen in public gardens in the middle of Athens or in small groups of trees in Istanbul as well as in London parks and suburban gardens.

It tends to feed more on the ground and in bushes, hedges and the lower branches of trees than the other tits. Although great tits are often present in the winter tit flocks, sometimes in considerable numbers, they are generally less gregarious than blue tits. When selecting a nest site the great tit is even more attracted to a nesting-box than the blue tit, though it would be an exaggeration to say that it never prefers a natural hole to a box.

The **BLUE TIT**, *Parus caeruleus*, is, in Britain, the best known of all the tit family. The fact that like jenny wren and robin redbreast it has been favoured with a 'christian name', as tom-tit, is an indication of its familiarity. A chunky, round-bodied bird with a short tail, it is easily distinguished from the other British species by its bright blue cap, bluish wings and tail and yellow underparts. The mantle, back and rump are greenish, and there is a bluish-grey line down the middle of the belly, though this is inconspicuous compared with the black band on the breast and belly of the great tit.

In the female the blues and yellows are generally less bright than in the male bird. Some males are conspicuously brilliant in colour and can be identified with confidence in the field, while a particularly dull bird will almost certainly be a female. There is also sometimes a visible difference in size between the sexes, as in the great tit, the male being the bigger bird: but there are many intermediate individuals which cannot safely be assigned to either sex by field observations of colour or size. The juvenile, before the autumn moult, has greenish upper parts, including the crown, and the cheeks, which are white in the adult, are yellow. A first-winter bird in the hand can be distinguished from one over a year old by its greenish, not pure blue, primary coverts and bastard wing.

The blue tit's vocabulary is not quite so extensive as the great tit's, nor as freely used, but it has a considerable variety of calls. Among the commonest are a high-pitched *tsee-tsee-tsee* and a scolding *churr*, softer and more slurred than the great tit's. The typical song begins with two or three single notes, *tsee, tsee*, which merge into a liquid trill.

The blue tit is almost as widely distributed in Europe as the great tit, but it does not extend as far north in Scandinavia or as far east in Asia, though it occurs in Asia Minor and Iran as well as north-west Africa and the Canaries. In the British Isles it has expanded its range during the present century by colonising the Isle of Man, the Isles of Scilly (in the late 1940s) and the Stornoway district of the Outer Hebrides (in 1963). Like the great tit it has pushed further north in Sutherland and Caithness. It does not breed in Orkney or Shetland. A few immigrants probably reach southern and eastern England every autumn and in some years there are large-scale irruptions.

Immigrants which have been critically examined have been shown to belong to the race *P. c. caeruleus* which covers practically the whole of continental Europe and has a greyish tinge on the upper parts. The British *P. c. obscurus* is slightly darker and greener on the back and less pure yellow on the underparts.

Like the great tit the blue tit breeds in a wide variety of woods and more open country as well as in gardens and occasional trees in suburbs and even in the middle of large cities. The differences between the two species in their choice of breeding habitat will be discussed in the next chapter. In winter blue tits feed regularly in conifer plantations as well as broad-leaved woodland, and unlike the other tits they often frequent reed-beds in large numbers. Many move into towns and villages in winter to feed at bird-tables.

In England blue tits are the most gregarious of the tits out of the breeding season. In the woods in winter they tend to feed more in the upper and outer twigs of trees than the other species, although they also search the bark and dead wood, especially in autumn. Their lightness and agility enable them to exploit foods like birch seed which are inaccessible to the heavier great tit. Blue tits often make use of nest-boxes but they are more likely than great tits to prefer a hole in a tree, wall or gate-post.

The **COAL TIT**, *Parus ater*, is the smallest British tit, and the difference in size is noticeable, especially when other species are present for comparison. The pattern of black and white on the head resembles the great tit's, but the conspicuous white patch on the nape distinguishes the coal tit from the other species. The whitish underparts without a central stripe also prevent confusion with the great tit. The olive-grey upper parts, whitish double wing bar and extensive black on the throat differentiate it from the marsh and willow tits. The short, slightly forked tail is also a diagnostic character.

The male bird usually has a slightly larger black patch on the throat and upper breast than the female, but the difference is not reliable enough to justify identification of the sexes in the field by plumage alone. In the juvenile, before the autumn moult, the nuchal patch, cheeks and underparts are yellowish, the cap sooty black, and there is only a small sooty patch on the chin. In the hand first-winter birds can be distinguished by the blue-grey inner feathers of the greater wing coverts: these feathers are yellow-brown in fully adult birds.

The coal tit's voice has a clear piping quality and lacks the nasal or metallic tone often heard in the utterances of the other members of the genus. The commonest call is a liquid *tsuee* or *seeseesee*. The song consists of the repetition of a phrase of two, or sometimes three, syllables, which might be represented as *weetser, teechu* or *teechuee*, or as the great tit's *tee-cher* song reversed to *cher-tee*.

The breeding range of the coal tit covers almost the whole of Europe except for the far north and limited areas in the south and east, and it extends eastwards across Asia to the Pacific and south to north-west Africa, Iran and the Himalayas. In the British Isles it is found almost wherever there are woods, and afforestation has enabled it to colonise the Scottish mainland to the extreme north, although it is absent from extensive treeless areas in the north-west and from Orkney and Shetland. Breeding was reported at Stornoway in 1966, but coal tits do not breed elsewhere in the Outer Hebrides. In spite of heavy losses in severe winters it is probably the most abundant tit in Scotland and it is particularly numerous in the old Caledonian pine forest. It breeds, rather sparsely, in the Isle of Man, but is only known as an occasional spring and autumn migrant in the Scillies. Forestry planting has enabled it to colonise new areas in Ireland, especially in the west, where it was not previously known. Immigrants to the British Isles occur chiefly in irruption years.

The continental race of the coal tit, *P. a. ater*, which ranges across Europe from France to Russia, has a pure blue-grey mantle, though northern birds tend to be more grey and to have less buff on the flanks. In the south the mantle is washed with olive and the flanks are more buff-coloured. A few specimens of the continental race have been identified in Britain, chiefly on the east coast.

The British race, *P. a. britannicus*, has the mantle washed with olive-buff, and the Irish, *P. a. hibernicus*, has a yellowish tinge on the under-parts and to a less extent on the cheeks and nuchal patch. However, coal tits from north-east Ireland, and some from the south and west, are indistinguishable from the British, while some specimens from South Wales are closely similar to the Irish type, and individuals with yellow tints are occasionally seen in north-west England.

Over most of its continental range the coal tit is almost exclusively a bird of coniferous forest, but in the Pyrenees, Cantabrian mountains, Apennines and Sardinia it is found also in broad-leaved woods. In the British Isles it is usually more abundant, and a more successful breeder, in conifer plantations than the other tits, but it also occurs widely, though rather unevenly, in deciduous woods and is one of the dominant species of the sessile oakwoods of hill country. It is a regular visitor to village and suburban gardens, but is scarce or absent in the centres of large urban areas.

The coal tit is generally gregarious except in the breeding season and is often present in some numbers in the mixed winter flocks. In conifers it searches for food in the needle clusters and opened cones. In broad-leaved woodland it will feed with blue and long-tailed tits among the twigs and buds of the canopy of the trees, but it spends more time than these species on the trunks and main branches extracting small insects and their eggs or pupae from crevices in the bark. It tends to nest in lower situations than the other tits: hollows under tree roots or boulders and holes in retaining walls of earth banks being favourite sites.

The **CRESTED TIT**, *Parus cristatus*, is easily distinguished from other species by its pointed crest, the black and white pattern on its crown and crest produced by white-edged black feathers, and its distinctive black and white facial pattern. In body plumage it resembles a rather drab marsh tit. The sexes are alike. Juveniles differ from adults in having a shorter crest with the feathers sooty brown and off-white and the black on throat and neck tinged with brown and a little less extensive.

The crested tit has a distinctive trilling call, and the normal form of song resembles a louder version of this trill. It also has a high-pitched contact note, *zee-zee-zee*, much like that of other tits.

It is widely distributed on the continent of Europe, though absent from most of Italy and Greece, and extends east to the Urals, but in the British Isles it is restricted, as a breeding species, to a limited area in north-east Scotland. It seems likely that 200 years ago it had a much wider range in Scotland than it has today. The felling of the old pine forests over much of the country destroyed its habitat, and at the beginning of this century it was practically confined to the remaining forest areas of the Spey valley in Inverness-shire. However, there has been some recovery of numbers and expansion of range in the last sixty years as a result of reafforestation, and crested tits now breed in five counties bordering the Moray Firth. There could be small pockets of breeding birds elsewhere in the Highlands, but there has been little sign of further spread in the last few years. D. Nethersole-Thompson has estimated the total Scottish population as rising to a maximum of 300–400 pairs after a succession of mild winters.

The race of the crested tit found in Scandinavia, west Russia and the Balkans, *P. c. cristatus*, has the upper parts greyish brown and the flanks washed with grey or buff. *P. c. scoticus*, the British native, is small and dark compared with continental birds. *P. c. mitratus*, from west and central Europe, is a warm buff-brown on the upper parts and rufous brown on the flanks. A few vagrants of the races *cristatus* and *mitratus* have reached the British Isles, usually in the south or east of England. They have been recorded as far north as Northumberland and as far west as the Isles of Scilly.

In Scotland the crested tit is almost exclusively a bird of the pine forest, although an admixture of birch and alder seems to be acceptable. In the greater part of Europe too this species is closely associated with conifers, but in central and southern France it is also found in deciduous woods with scattered evergreens, and in Spain it nests in cork oak forests as well as among pines.

In autumn crested tits may join, in small numbers, with mixed flocks of great, blue and coal tits, goldcrests and treecreepers, but in general they resemble marsh tits in their sedentary, territorial habits. They feed among the needles and twigs of pine trees at all heights and also search for food on the trunks and on the ground. The commonest nest site is a roughly excavated hole in the rotten trunk or stump of a tree.

The **MARSH TIT**, *Parus palustris*, is by no means a brightly coloured bird, with its black cap, grey-brown back and off-white cheeks and underparts, but at all times of year it gives the impression of being meticulously well-groomed and elegant. It has a longer tail than the coal tit and lacks the latter's white wing bars and white nuchal stripe. It is much more difficult to distinguish by sight from the willow tit, but in a good light and at close range the gloss on the cap of the adult marsh tit, the whitish flanks and the lack of a pale patch on the wing are diagnostic. Individual variations within the species are usually small, but occasional marsh tits show a light-coloured patch on the secondaries, and this may lead to confusion with willow tits. The sexes are alike. Juveniles have duller caps, greyer backs and whiter underparts than adults.

When visible differences between two species are so slight vocal distinctions are especially important. The marsh tit has two common and characteristic calls that are never used by the willow tit. They can be verbalised with reasonable accuracy as *pitchew* and *chickadee-dee*, both sometimes used with an extra syllable. A harsh *tchaa-tchaa* might be confused with the willow tit's *tchay* but is less deep and grating and is usually preceded by a *pitchew* call. The commonest form of song, which is sometimes strikingly loud and resonant, consists of the repetition of a single note: *chip-chip-chip*, but a disyllabic form, *chippi-chippi-chippi*, is also frequently used, and there are occasional variations with three or four syllables.

The marsh tit has a rather more restricted range in Europe than most tit species. It breeds from Britain and the Pyrenees east to the Urals, north to southern Scandinavia and south to Italy and the Balkans. In Asia the marsh tit is found locally from Turkey to China and Burma. In the British Isles it is not found in Ireland, although attempts have been made to introduce it there, and in Scotland it is only recorded from a limited area in Berwickshire and, since 1966, Roxburgh. It is scarce in west Cornwall and parts of Wales and it has not been recorded on the Isles of Scilly. There are no breeding records for the Isle of Man, but a marsh or willow tit frequented a bird-table on the island from 1969 to 1971. In north-west England the marsh tit is abundant in the limestone woodlands of south Westmorland and not uncommon in the oakwoods of the southern half of the Lake District, but it is a rare bird north of the watershed through the middle of the Cumbrian mountains.

The continental race of the marsh tit, *P. p. palustris*, is a little paler and greyer than the British *P. p. dresseri*. Birds from north-west France are more like the British form. There is no conclusive evidence that continental birds cross to Britain.

The marsh tit is more definitely a woodland bird than the great or blue tits, and it is even less inclined than the coal tit to colonise suburbia, but it does visit gardens and orchards in more rural surroundings and it can be tamed to hand-feeding as easily as other species. Most books describe it as a bird of deciduous woods, and indeed it is rarely found in pure conifer plantations, but its close association with yew trees seems to have been overlooked. Like the great tit the marsh is a hammering tit, and at least in the limestone woods on the southern fringe of the English Lake District yew-seed kernels seem to be the staple diet for both these species through the winter. The reference to marshes in both the English and scientific names is misleading, as more often than not the bird is found in dry woodlands. The name was, of course, established before the willow tit, which does have some preference for marshy situations, was recognised as a separate species. However, the marsh tit also occurs quite commonly among willows and alders on marshy ground or on the banks of streams, and it should not be assumed that a black-capped tit seen in this kind of habitat is more likely to be a willow than a marsh.

Compared with blue and coal tits the marsh tit is more often seen in bushes or low branches of trees than in the canopy, though it does not feed on the ground as much as the great tit. In autumn it is often seen on the seed-heads of marsh thistle and knapweed. Marsh tits are much less gregarious than the species described above, and after the family parties have dispersed in late summer it is unusual to see more than two or three in the mixed winter flocks. The nest is usually built in a natural hole in a tree, rather low down, but in some districts holes in stone walls or banks are commonly used.

The **WILLOW TIT**, *Parus montanus*, was not recognised as a separate species from the marsh tit until the end of the nineteenth century, and bird books published before the beginning of the present century usually attribute to the marsh tit details of distribution and behaviour that clearly refer to the willow tit. The plumage differences between the two are slight. At least in winter the most obvious distinguishing character of the willow tit is the light-coloured patch on the closed wing caused by the pale edging to the secondaries, but this is less noticeable in summer and, as mentioned above, occasional marsh tits show similar pale wing markings. The dull, sooty, loose-feathered cap of the willow tit is visibly different from the sleek, glossy crown of the marsh tit at close quarters, but one needs a good view of the bird to be sure of this distinction.

Other minor differences are that the willow tit has browner flanks than the marsh, the black cap extends further down the nape, and the blackish chin patch is a little larger but less sharply defined than the marsh tit's. In the hand, willow tits can be distinguished from marsh tits by the fact that their outer tail feathers are shorter than the inner ones, a difference that is visible in the nestlings when they are a fortnight old. The sexes are alike, and the juveniles are hardly distinguishable in the field from young marsh tits.

It must be admitted that for sight identification the marsh and willow tits can be almost as difficult a pair of species as the willow warbler and the chiffchaff, and my notebooks contain not infrequent records of 'marlow tits' (as the widely used 'comic tern' for an unidentified common or arctic tern). A good view of the generally less common willow tit often makes its identity immediately unmistakable, with the main characters (a matt, velvety cap, light wing patch and brownish flanks) all clearly visible, but the last two of these are less obvious in some individuals than in others, and at any time a silent black-capped tit overhead or at a distance can present a problem.

Willow tits are much easier to identify by sound than by sight, though unfortunately for the observer they are generally less vocal than the other members of the genus. There are two forms of song: a clear, penetrating *piu-piu-piu*, and a much more elaborate and untitlike combination of some high-pitched notes with liquid ones of almost nightingale or garden-warbler quality. The latter form is rarely heard, and even the commoner and simpler type is used chiefly in competition with a close neighbour, so that the male of an isolated pair may never be heard singing at all. The most striking utterance of the species is a loud, harsh, low-pitched call, usually, though inadequately, written as *tchay*. A feeding and contact note, a nasal *eez-eez-eez*, is also distinctive. Either of these calls may be preceded by two or three notes which sound like *chick, chick*.

The breeding range of the willow tit in Europe is more northerly and easterly than that of other British tits; it is absent from large parts of the west and south of the continent. Its range extends eastwards across Asia to the Pacific, north to the tree line and south to the Kirghiz Steppes, Mongolia and Japan. It probably breeds in every county of England and Wales except Anglesey. In a few districts, such as parts of Cheshire, south Yorkshire, west Suffolk and Hertford-shire, it outnumbers the marsh tit, but over most of the country it is much less abundant and there are considerable areas, especially in north-west and south-west England, where it is rare or absent. It has not been recorded in the Scillies or, with one possible exception, in the Isle of Man. The willow tit is not found in Ireland, but in Scotland replaces the marsh tit except in the extreme south-east. Before 1950 there were records as far north as Ross-shire, and at the end of the nineteenth century a black-capped tit, presumed to have been the willow tit, seems to have been fairly plentiful in the Spey valley. It now appears to have deserted the Highlands altogether and also some of its former haunts in south-west Scotland.

The British race of the willow tit, *P. m. kleinschmidti*, is smaller, darker and browner than the continental races. The Scandinavian bird, *P. m. borealis*, has greyer back and wings and conspicuously white cheeks, a difference noticeable in the field. Birds believed to be of this race have been recorded twice in England and once on Fair Isle.

In choice of habitat the willow tit does not differ greatly from the marsh tit, at least in Britain. The willow tit's apparent preference for swampy ground is probably due to the abundance there of the rotten tree stumps or trunks which provide nest sites, but it is also found in dry woodland, and it is not uncommon to find marsh and willow tits as close neighbours in the same wood. Both occur in the elder un-derstorey of coverts and shelter-belts. In many parts of Europe the willow tit is, as its scientific name implies, a bird of mountainside woodland, both deciduous and coniferous. In Britain, too, willow tits —unlike marsh tits—are found in conifer plantations. The willow tit is less of a garden bird than the marsh, but it does sometimes visit bird-tables in rural surroundings or outer suburbs. It finds its food chiefly among bushes and the lower branches of trees or in the herb layer. Dr Bruce Campbell remarks that it dives into low cover, apparently to feed as well as to hide, much more than the other tit species. It has a slightly longer and finer bill than the marsh tit and this suggests that it may be adapted to a diet of small insects rather than hard seeds.

Unlike the marsh tit the willow normally excavates its own nest-hole in a rotten stump or trunk. The nest is very slight, a thin pad of fur, hair and perhaps a few feathers; it lacks the thick foundation of moss usually found in a marsh tit's nest.

Three other tits of the genus *Parus* breed in continental Europe but have not yet been definitely identified in the British Isles. The **AZURE TIT**, *P. cyanus*, replaces the blue tit in eastern Europe and central Asia, and as vagrants have appeared in Holland and France it might eventually occur in Britain. It is larger than a blue tit and has a blue-grey back and white underparts, and the adults have white crowns. The **SIBERIAN** or **LAPP TIT**, *P. cinctus*, a bird of the conifer and birch forests of Scandinavia and Russia, resembles a large dusty-looking willow tit with brown crown, nape and throat patch. The **SOMBRE TIT**, *P. lugubris*, found in the Balkans and Asia Minor, is a large sturdily built tit with plumage like a marsh tit's but with a much larger black throat patch.

The **LONG-TAILED TIT**, *Aegithalos caudatus*, has always been placed in a separate genus from the *Parus* tits, but it was, until about twenty years ago, regarded as a member of the tit family, the Paridae, and this relationship is recognised by its vernacular name in most, if not all, European languages. Indeed the question whether the long-tailed tit should be regarded as belonging to a separate family from the *Parus* tits or only to a sub-family within the Paridae is still open to discussion. Certainly long-tailed tits are found in association with other tits throughout the greater part of the year over almost the whole of Europe, so it seems natural to conclude this chapter with some notes on them.

Mistaken identification of an adult long-tailed tit is almost impossible even on a distant view. A 3 inch (7½cm) graduated tail attached to a 2½ inch (6½cm) body gives the bird an outline that is almost unique among European species: the larger bearded tit's colouring and habitat are so different that confusion is unlikely. The pattern of the long-tailed tit's loose-textured black, white and pink plumage is also distinctive. The sexes are alike, but young birds have shorter tails and dark cheeks and they lack the pink tints on the back and underparts.

One regular contact call of a party moving through trees is a thin *zee-zee-zee*, similar to, though not identical with, that of *Parus* tits. A low *tupp* and a trilling *tsirr* are also constantly used and are entirely distinctive. The song, infrequently heard, seems to consist of a combination of call notes.

The long-tailed tit is absent from the far north of Scandinavia and Russia but otherwise is found throughout continental Europe and across central Asia. It breeds throughout Great Britain and Ireland, including the Isle of Man, with the exception of Caithness, the Northern Isles, the Outer Hebrides and the Isles of Scilly. Its numbers are much affected by severe winter weather, but recovery is usually rapid and after a succession of mild winters the long-tailed tit is a fairly common bird in many parts of Britain.

The north-eastern race of the long-tailed tit *Aegithalos caudatus caudatus*, which extends from Norway and Sweden through Poland to the Ukraine, has a pure white head and a black upper mantle. Several individuals of this type have been reported in the British Isles. The British race, *A. c. rosaceus*, has dark longitudinal lines on the head.

In the breeding season the long-tailed tit is a bird of hedgerows, thickets, scrub and woodland edges rather than the forest, though it is found in more open parts of both broad-leaved and coniferous woods, and commonly in the thicket stage of plantations. In winter it is more often seen in mature woodland, either in unmixed parties or in association with mixed tit flocks. The long-tailed tits tend to move faster, and probably further, than the other tit species. They sometimes visit bird-tables in rural areas or outer suburbs and they have recently nested in central London parks, but they are not often seen in the more closely built-up parts of large towns.

A male great tit displaying aggressively

The domed oval nest (plate, p 101), constructed of moss, lichen and cobwebs with an abundant lining of feathers, is most commonly placed in a low gorse or thorn bush or a dense hedge, but some nests are built in completely open positions in the fork of a branch or trunk of a tree up to 70 feet above the ground. The cryptic effect of the moss and lichen and the shape of the nest is striking in these situations, and it has been suggested that high tree nests are the ancestral type and the low ones are an adaptation to a comparatively recent adoption of a hedge and bush habitat.

A blue tit with its crest raised, a sign of anxiety or indecision

3 The Preliminaries of the Breeding Cycle

There are four basic pre-requisites for successful reproduction by any of the *Parus* tits: the choice of a favourable breeding habitat, the establishment of a territory, the formation of a stable pair-bond, and the selection and defence of a nest-site. The four conditions are not necessarily fulfilled in the same order for all pairs of tits, and the period over which the preparations extend is highly variable. They are often noticeable before the end of December, especially near houses, but may then lapse for days or weeks in severe winter weather and be resumed in a more intense and active form in February or March.

HABITAT

Whether a pair of tits eventually raises a big family, a small one or no fledglings at all will largely depend upon the choice of a suitable environment for the nest. A site must be available, either a ready-made hole or, for some species, a rotten tree-trunk or branch which can easily be excavated. Plantations of young healthy trees, whether broad-leaved or coniferous, lack both holes and rotten wood, and it is only when nest-boxes are supplied that hole-nesting birds can colonise such woods in any numbers. A lavish distribution of boxes in a wood may sometimes produce an abnormally high population of great tits, which are specially attracted by them, but in general nest-boxes placed in commercially managed woodland are only compensating for the tree-holes that would be abundantly available in natural uncleared forest.

The other necessity for a favourable breeding habitat is an adequate supply of food for the growing young. A plantation or garden that provides good feeding for adult tits in winter, small invertebrates, seeds, buds, catkins or human largesse, does not necessarily produce in May and June a sufficient quantity of the moth larvae which form the staple diet of the nestlings; when the birds choose their territories in early spring they have to anticipate conditions two or three months ahead if they are to achieve maximum breeding success. There is strong evidence that there is much competition for territories in the kind of habitat which produces most food for nestlings; for example, great, blue and marsh tits seek out woods with well-grown oak trees.

Even casual observation will show marked differences in the habitat preferences of some of the tit species, but a more precise indication is given by comparing the actual breeding populations in different kinds of woodland. The Common Birds Census of the British Trust for Ornithology is accumulating valuable data on these lines, but any reliable method of making a complete count of breeding birds in woodland requires many man-hours of observation, so there are still only a limited number of woods for which complete bird-population figures are available. In order to compare the population density in various kinds of woodland in different regions a quicker sampling method is needed. A technique that has been widely used by two authorities on woodland birds, W. B. Yapp and Eric Simms, is that of the 'line transect'.[1] The observer walks through a wood at a speed of 2 miles (3·2km) an hour and records all the birds seen or heard on the way. The 'relative abundance' of each species is then obtained by expressing the number of 'contacts' with that species as a percentage of the total contacts with birds of all species. As more contacts are made by sound than by sight, the numbers of the more vocal and easily audible species may be over-estimated, but this applies to some extent to other counting methods.

Table 1 illustrates the wide range of broad-leaved woods frequented by great and blue tits and their generally similar abundance in them, but there are some noteworthy regional differences, for instance the scarcity of the great tit in sessile oak woods in Scotland and in birch woods in England and Wales. In some cases the species of the domi-

TABLE I   RELATIVE ABUNDANCE OF 4 TIT SPECIES IN
WOODS IN SUMMER

	No of woods	Author	Great tit	Blue tit	Coal tit	Marsh tit
Pedunculate oak, England	88	Simms	4	5		
Sessile oak, England and Wales	36	Simms	3	2	5	
Scotland	10	Simms		8		
Alder, Scotland	6	Simms	3	5		
Beech, England	16	Simms	8	5		2
Scotland	6	Simms	3	9		
Birch, England and Wales	13	Yapp		4		
N Scotland	26	Yapp	2	2	3	
Ash, England and Wales	13	Yapp	4	3		2
Scots pine, N and E Scotland	12	Simms			17	
Norway spruce, Scotland	6	Simms	1		4	

nant trees may have less significance than their age and size or the composition of the shrub layer. Thus great tits, with their habit of searching for food on tree trunks or on the ground, tend to prefer old and open woodland; blue tits feed chiefly among leaves and twigs, and are usually more abundant in damp riverside situations whatever the prevalent tree species may be. Both species are normally scarce in spring in British conifer plantations, but great tits can be induced by nest-boxes to breed in them in fair numbers. However, their population density is still lower than in broad-leaved woods, and nestlings of early broods not infrequently die of starvation. Blue tits are more reluctant to breed in conifer woods even with nest-boxes and their early broods are also often unsuccessful.

Great and blue tits are much less restricted to woodland than the other species and may breed in any habitat offering nest-sites and a few trees or large bushes. In particular both species nest in town parks and gardens, though the blue tit is generally the commoner bird in built-up areas. Some of the blue tits that gather round garden feeding-stations in winter move out into the woods to breed, but many others select nest-sites close to houses, even though the generally small clutches and poor fledging success of tits in small town gardens suggest that these are an unfavourable breeding habitat. Some blue and great tits may be attracted to gardens by nest-boxes, others seem simply to prefer to nest close to houses, even in natural holes. Of tit nests found in a large rural area of south Cumbria and north Lancashire, during a recent survey, 52 per cent of the blue tit nests, 39 per cent of the great tit nests, 33 per cent of the coal tit nests, but none of the marsh tit nests were found within 25 yards of occupied houses. Indeed, some of the blue tits were observed making regular flights of over 200 yards from a nest in a wall of a building to collect food in woods where suitable tree holes were available.

Throughout much the greater part of its Eurasian range the coal tit is closely associated with coniferous forest, and in Britain too it is the most abundant tit species both in the old pine forests of northern Scotland and in modern conifer plantations. In the British Isles and a few parts of southern and western Europe the coal tit also breeds in broad-leaved woods, and it is actually the most numerous of the tits in many woods of sessile oak in the hill country of Wales and northern England, though not in those of Scotland. A. J. Deadman finds it the most abundant tit in the birchwoods of north-east Scotland.[2] In deciduous woods in lowland parts of England, coal tits are wide-spread but generally not numerous. For example in a wood of about 80 hectares, mainly of pedunculate oak, in Northamptonshire, Eric Simms found 2 pairs of coal tits annually for five years, compared with averages of 20 pairs of great tits, 31·4 pairs of blue tits and 5·2 pairs of marsh tits.

In view of the species' apparent preference for conifers it seems surprising that Dr J. A. Gibb and Dr Monica Betts found that coal tits lay larger clutches of eggs and rear more young per pair in broad-leaved woods than in conifers.[3] The authors' conclusion is that coal tits, the smallest of the *Parus* species, 'are only adapted to life in pine in so far as they are better able to survive interspecific competition there than in broad-leaved woods, perhaps because their small size and fine beak enable them to take advantage of the very small prey prevailing in the pine in winter. Coal tits may be described as pine-tolerant rather than pine-loving.' W. B. Yapp has suggested that they breed among conifers because the sparse vegetation underneath exposes suitable nest-holes in the ground. Mountainside oak woods also provide abundant nest sites under roots and rocks. The sandy soils of East Anglian Breckland conifer plantations do not seem favourable for ground nesting, yet coal tits are abundant there and readily occupy nest-boxes placed on the trees.

On the whole it seems likely that the coal tit was originally a bird of the pine and birch forest and has adapted itself to life in some kinds of broad-leaved woodland. Dr D. W. Snow has shown that in the *Parus* tits the form of the beak of each species is correlated with its habitat.[4] Tits which feed in broad-leaved trees have short thick beaks while those that feed in conifers have comparatively long fine ones. This is clearly shown in the following table, compiled by Lack from Snow's data, in which the last column gives an effective index of comparative thickness of bill.[5] The crested tit, which is almost entirely restricted to conifers, has the finest bill, the coal tit next, and the blue tit, a bird of broad-leaved woods, the thickest. Great and willow tits, which are found in both habitats, have intermediate bills. The difference in length and shape between the beaks of blue tits and those of crested and coal tits is noticeable in the field.

TABLE 2   TYPICAL WEIGHTS AND MEASUREMENTS OF MALE TITS

	Weight gm	Wing length mm	Culmen (beak length) mm	Beak depth mm	Depth ÷ culmen
Coal tit	9·3	60	10·8	3·7	0·35
Blue tit	11·4	64	9·3	4·4	0·47
Great tit	20·0	76	13·0	5·2	0·40
Willow tit	10·1	60	10·6	4·0	0·38
Marsh tit	11·4	63	10·4	4·3	0·41
Crested tit (Scandinavian specimens)	11·0	64	11·5	3·6	0·31

It has been suggested that a long thin bill is adapted to small food items, and Monica Betts found that the insects taken in English pine plantations are smaller than those taken in oak woods. But the long-tailed tit, admittedly of a different genus, also takes very small food items and yet has a conspicuously short stubby bill. An alternative theory is that a fine beak is better adapted for extracting insects from clusters of pine needles. It should also be more effective in picking pine and spruce seed, a food often stored for winter use, out of the opening cones.

Although the crested tit is sometimes found in broad-leaved woods in parts of southern Europe it is practically confined to coniferous forest over most of its range. The Scottish crested tit is indeed much more specialised in its habitat requirements than any other British tit. It breeds among the old Scots pines of the Caledonian Forest, and the birch, rowan and alder in the more open parts of the forest seem to be of little significance to it, except for offering possible nest-sites. Crested tits are slowly colonising younger plantations of pines, and more rarely of spruce and Douglas fir, but the populations seem to be restricted by the scarcity of nest-holes or of dead wood in which they can be excavated. One or two pairs have recently been breeding in nest-boxes in Culbin Forest, Morayshire, but the boxes cannot yet be said to affect the numbers of crested tits in the young planta-tions.[6]

Marsh tits are more closely restricted to broad-leaved woodland than any of the other British tits, but even they are not averse to a certain admixture of conifers, and they regularly join coal tits in ex-tracting pine seed from cones in April and May. A favourite habitat is ash or pedunculate oak with an understorey of hazel or elder, but marsh tits are also quite common in beech and birch woods as well as in waterside alders and willows. In most of these woods, however, they are greatly outnumbered by great and blue tits and so fail to qualify for inclusion in the table of Relative Abundance (page 38). Marsh tits are not found in the high-level sessile oak woods in the north of England, but are not uncommon in the lower oak woods of the southern Lake District and are abundant where oak is mixed with yew on the limestone hills. They also breed in old orchards and large wooded gardens, but not often very near houses. Colour-ringed birds that have frequented bird-tables through the winter often retire to the wood in March or April and return in late summer.

The willow tit does not appear at all in the tables of Relative Abundance prepared by Yapp and Simms, a fair indication of its generally thin distribution in the British Isles. Over most of its continental range the willow tit is a bird of birches and coniferous forest, a habitat in which it used to be found in the Caledonian Forest of Speyside until some twenty years ago. In Britain now it breeds in a wide range of woodlands, including conifer plantations, pedunculate oak, willow and alder and mixed broad-leaved woods. Both willow and marsh tits prefer a rich shrub layer and tend to avoid open park-like conditions, but marsh tits are nearly always the more numerous of the two when they occur together. For example, in 1949 Marley Wood, near Oxford, a very mixed broad-leaved wood of 22 hectares, had a population of about 30 pairs of great tits, 40 of blue tits, 8 of marsh tits, 2 or 3 of coal tits and long-tailed tits and 2 of willow tits.[7]

In twenty- to thirty-year-old plantations of Scots and Corsican pine in Thetford Chase, East Anglia, J. A. Gibb estimated the breeding population of willow tits and long-tailed tits at 'probably 6–15 birds per 100 hectares', compared with 1–5 birds per 100 hectares for great and blue tits, more than 35 for coal tits, and no marsh tits.[8] Willow tits occasionally used nest-boxes in these plantations, so perhaps the attraction of an uncrowded environment outweighed the lack of normal nest-sites.

Damp birch woods are a favourite habitat of willow tits throughout England, Wales and southern Scotland. Six or more pairs of willow tits habitually nest in one such wood of only 5·6 hectares in south-west Scotland. The absence of marsh and coal tits may partly account for this local abundance, but the numerous rotten birch trunks, so easily excavated, must be a major attraction. The absence of willow tits from many similar birch woods in other parts of Britain is difficult to explain, but the fact that they are sometimes evicted by great and blue tits from holes they have excavated shows that interspecific competition is not necessarily limited to food. Pressure from large populations of the bigger and more aggressive tit species might account for the generally thin distribution of the willow tit in Britain.

Long-tailed tits breed in a wide variety of woods, both broad-leaved and coniferous, but they generally prefer the clearings and woodland edges, or hedgerows and thickets away from the woods. Nesting in either dense bush or high tree-fork, long-tailed tits are not likely to be restricted in their choice of breeding habitat, but they do seem to be specially attracted by certain types of site, for example blackthorn thickets, and this could affect their local distribution.

TERRITORY

The 'territory' of birds and animals has been defined simply as 'any defended area', but the form of territory relevant here is the area defended against birds of the same species during the breeding season or in preparation for it. The defence may take the form of song, which often serves as a warning to other birds of the occupation of a territory, or of threatening postures, attack or pursuit. The element of defence distinguishes territory from the 'range' within which many tits feed during the winter and often spend their whole lives.

All the *Parus* tits hold breeding territories, but they vary in how they are established and how long they are maintained. In late summer and early autumn there is a temporary outburst of 'reproductive behaviour': this may include song, territorial display and fighting, a tendency for paired birds to keep company and visit nest-holes, and sometimes the formation of new pairs among juveniles. This activity tends to lapse in early winter, and the serious establishment of breeding territories comes after the winter lull.

Professor R. A. Hinde found that in Marley Wood, near Oxford, great tits formed pairs within the winter flock, each pair gradually spending more time in a 'preferred area' in the wood, especially in the early morning, and the male singing there.[9] At first a fluid region round the preferred stations was defended against neighbours, and more vigorously against strangers. The territory was not associated with any particular nest-site and display took place at many different holes. The boundaries were never precise but were most clearly defined during the nest-building period. Territorial activity dwindled during the incubation and nestling periods, but there was some recurrence of it just before the young left the nest.

Professor Hinde found generally similar behaviour among blue tits in this wood, with pairs showing increasing preference for a particular area which later became a defended territory. But with some blue tits the attraction of a particular nest-site seems to play an important part, and the nest-hole rather than a 'preferred area' forms the nucleus of the territory. For example, in the winter of 1970–1 a male blue tit roosted regularly in a certain nest-box in my garden. During January he became increasingly aggressive towards other tits in the vicinity, attacking them up to 10 yards from the box. He also began visiting the box several times during the day and could be heard hammering at the inside for some time after going to roost. Early in February he allowed another colour-ringed blue tit to perch on twigs outside the box. She eventually became his mate, taking over the box for roosting early in April, and it was only then that territorial disputes developed with neighbours about 20 yards away. At another box, not used for roosting, a male sang persistently from 25 February, and drove other small birds out of his tree. There was no sign of a mate until early April and no territorial activity more than a few yards from the home tree before then. Some male great tits will also sing assiduously near a particular nest-hole in early spring some weeks before acquiring a mate or defending a territory. This kind of mating behaviour is more like that of other hole-nesting birds such as the pied flycatcher.[10]

In his study of coal tits in conifer plantations in Morayshire, A. J. Deadman found that although some first-winter coal tits are paired before they acquire a territory, in other cases the male claims a territory and advertises for a mate by song. A pair of adults surviving from the previous year will return to their former territory, and a surviving male will also return to his home ground and obtain a new mate, but a widowed female may move some distance away. First-winter males began to defend a small area in January and territories were usually established in their final form in March.

There is little evidence of territorial behaviour among great, blue or coal tits between the fledging of the young and the temporary recrudescence in the autumn, but marsh tits' territory is normally maintained, with only minor adjustments, throughout the year. If one of a pair dies the survivor holds the territory until a new partner is found. It is defended throughout the year against neighbouring marsh tits, although passing flocks of tits, including landless marsh tits, are accepted without opposition. Some juvenile marsh tits form pairs and claim territories in their first autumn. Some willow tits associate in pairs on the breeding territory throughout the year. Crested tits also are found in pairs all the year round and their sedentary habits have been confirmed by observation of ringed birds.[11]

Very often the first and most obvious sign of territorial activity among passerine birds is song—though this does not imply that the only function of song is the claiming of territory: it also maintains contact between the pair and may have other uses as well. In the tit family both species and individuals differ widely in their use of song. The most noticeable and assiduous singer is the great tit. In woods regular song usually begins in January, but in town and suburban gardens even in the north of England great tits frequently sing in December and may begin in November. This early start might be attributed to the tendency of garden great tits to remain in their breeding territories through the winter, and this in turn could be due to an easy localised food supply on bird-tables. It is only in July, August and the first half of November that song is uncommon in an urban environment. The singing activity of a particular male may be affected to some extent by the weather and by his own internal condition, perhaps including the need for rest after a period of intense song, but a bird is often roused to respond to the singing of others. Terry Gompertz showed that this rivalry induces a singing great tit to copy the rhythm and tempo of his competitor, and this may lead to the temporary local prevalence of certain less common song types, for instance the three-note variety.[12] There is also a tendency, more marked in some in-dividuals than others, to change from one to another of the usual repertoire of four to seven song types, apparently to avoid monotony. Miss Gompertz found that first-year males in spring 'seem to experi-ment, missing a beat here or putting in a note there, until there emerges a pattern which appears to satisfy them'. Apart from the great tit's song, its well-known *tink* call, normally only used by males, has a clear territorial significance. It is used by a bird when first establishing a territory, or sometimes in answer to a neighbour's song.

Blue tits, which often use a conspicuous display flight, generally seem to rely less upon song to advertise territorial claims than do great tits. Indeed some males only sing very infrequently even during the egg-laying period. Other males are assiduous singers near their nest-holes in the earlier stages of the breeding cycle. One with an injured wing kept indoors for some days in April sang most persistently from the top of his vase of twigs. But it is certainly true that most blue tits are less regular singers than most great tits and their range of audibility is smaller. The typical song is much more stereotyped than the great tit's; it lasts about a second and may be repeated twenty times or more in a minute. Alternative songs, including a version of the great tit's *see-saw*, are occasionally heard. Song is frequent from January to June but is only occasionally heard in the second half of the year.

Coal tits are particularly responsive to the singing activity of their neighbours. Two rivals on the border of their respective territories sometimes sing almost throughout the day, but the male of an isolated pair may sing little if at all. There are also regional differences. In East Anglian pine plantations J. A. Gibb was able to plot coal tit territories over a considerable area from two half-hour listening periods, and in the Netherlands L. Tinbergen recorded about 7·5 songs per hour in his study area. But in the Culbin Forest on the Moray Firth, Dr Myles Crooke heard only one song per hour although coal tits were breeding in greater density there than in the Dutch woods.[13] Coal tits may be heard singing in any month, but spring song normally begins in January and reaches a maximum in March and April. There is little territorial song between the beginning of incubation and the dispersal of family parties in June, although the male may sing softly to call his mate off the nest. Both adults and juveniles sing during the late summer and early autumn, but there is a lull in the moulting period and during cold weather in late autumn and winter.

As marsh and willow tits are small woodland birds with inconspicuous and closely similar plumage it is not surprising that their typical songs are loud, clear and distinctive. Marsh tits up to 150 yards apart answer each other's songs, and they may use a repertoire of three or four different song types. What is surprising is that birds which maintain a territory throughout the year, as most marsh tits and apparently some willow tits do, should only sing for such a small part of it. Marsh tits only sing regularly from mid-January to the end of April, with a marked peak in February and March, although in summer and autumn juveniles sometimes intersperse bursts of 'song' with other calls. However, at all times of year the familiar *pitchou* call may be used, apparently more often by the male than the female, as a declaration of territorial rights, and in spring it may serve to answer a neighbour's song. It is not used by landless birds in the flock. The willow tit's song period is rather more extended than the marsh tit's, but singing, especially the warbler type, is generally infrequent. It may be that the *tchay* call serves some of the same purposes as the marsh tit's *pitchou* or the great tit's *tink*.

The crested tit, an inconspicuous, cryptically plumaged small bird living in evergreen trees, might be expected also to have a loud distinctive song. In fact observers who have spent much time watching crested tits have failed to distinguish a song at all, apart from the multi-purpose purring trill, though Dr Stuart Smith described a song 'not unlike that of a blue tit . . . *zee, zee, zee cheera cheera*'.[14] A high-pitched double note has also been described and 'an exceedingly rare liquid utterance'. The long-tailed tit is another very infrequent singer, and its occasional bubbling medley is chiefly composed of the familiar call notes. It does not appear to defend a breeding territory.[15]

Two general features of the songs of tits should be mentioned. One is the scope for variation found in the songs of most species, especially great, coal and marsh tits. This allows each singer to develop an individuality in his song that will be easily recognisable both to his mate and his neighbours. Diversification also seems to have an intrinsic appeal to the performer. The other is the fact that singing by female great, blue, coal, marsh and willow tits has been reported, whereas in most passerine genera female song is exceptional or unknown. Genuine song by female tits is probably not common, and when it does occur it is usually associated with active territorial defence; but, as so often in the tit family, there are occasional individuals which do not follow the general rule. One of Miss Howard's hand-tamed female great tits had a distinctive song 'much superior to the male's' and sang it in several successive nesting seasons.

It is clear that singing plays an important part in the establishment and demarcation of territory, but there are times when it is supplemented or replaced by 'reproductive fighting'. The simplest form of this is the 'supplanting attack', in which one bird, nearly always a

male, flies directly at its rival and usually drives it away. This is sometimes followed by a chase which may involve females as well as males.
Often, however, a border encounter leads to the adoption by both
male birds of threatening postures which are more stereotyped in
some species than in others. The 'reproductive threat display' is most
highly developed in the great tit. In the typical 'head-up' display, two
cocks face each other, or turn partly away, with the body almost
vertical, the bill pointing upwards and the head turning from side to
side (plate, page 33). The wings are held close to the flanks and the
body looks sleek and slim. The effect of this display is to show off
the black gorget and contrasting white cheeks to the rival. This does
not necessarily mean that the colour pattern was evolved to fit the
posture, or *vice versa*, but it is noticeable that the other tits use this
position less often and in a less developed form. It is sometimes used
in territorial disputes by coal tits, which also have black throats and
white cheeks, occasionally by blue tits, but only in a momentary
approximation by marsh tits. The 'horizontal' threat display of the
great tit (plate, page 120), in which the wings and tail are widely spread,
the rump feathers fluffed and the bill pointed either downwards or
towards the adversary, is normally used against competitors for food
(see Chapter 12) and only rarely in territorial disputes; but this posture
seems to be the basis of a territorial threat display by the marsh tit,
which points its bill down and thus shows off its glossy black crown.
Tits in territorial conflict also use a wide range of positions and
modifications of the set of the feathers, including crouching, flicking,
drooping or raising the wings, cocking up or spreading the tail and
fluffing or sleeking various parts of the head and body plumage.
One attitude may follow another in rapid succession, probably re-
flecting changes of mood and the ebb and flow of aggression and fear.
A sort of aerial threat display sometimes adopted by most, if not all,
of the *Parus* species consists of a curious flight with the body unnaturally upright and the wings beating rapidly.

These conflicts are accompanied by characteristic calls. Great and
blue tits of both sexes use a form of the *churr* and male great tits utter
what Miss Gompertz aptly called a 'muttered threat'. Marsh tits have
a variety of threat notes and 'battle-cries', and coal tits pursue each other
with excited high-pitched calls.

Female tits sometimes join actively in disputes with neighbours, but in most species it is unusual for the female's participation to go beyond vocal support for her mate. The contests rarely result in any injury to the birds, but on 4 May 1958 Mrs J. Hall-Craggs found one coal tit killing another by hammering at its scalp and nape. The rescued victim died within four minutes.

It is these border incidents which chiefly determine the boundaries, and to some degree the area, of neighbouring territories. If a pair of tits has no close neighbours of the same species the boundaries remain vague, but territories are still not of unlimited size. Mated tits tend to sing, display, roost and feed within a limited area even if there is no competition from others of the same species, and they may leave large parts of a wood unoccupied and unvisited. But in a desirable habitat the size of a territory will probably be reduced by pressure from other pairs. In Marley Wood the territories of great tits averaged 0·8 hectares, while in a rather poor mixed wood in the Netherlands the average was 2–2·8 hectares. Blue tits in Marley had territories of from 0·2 to 0·8 hectares, and marsh tits 1·5–2·2 hectares.[16] Willow tits seem to be exceptionally mobile and wide-ranging, and where their population density is low their territories are surprisingly large, for example about 10 and 14 hectares for the two pairs in Marley Wood. Territories must have been much smaller in the Scottish birchwood of 5·6 hectares with six pairs of willow tits. In Scottish conifer plantations coal tits had territories varying from 1·4 to 11·3 hectares.

Defence of territory is so widespread among many families of birds, and makes such demands upon their time and energy, that one might expect it to produce some striking and obvious advantage for the species. It has been claimed that territorial behaviour limits the population density of each species practising it and ensures even spacing over the available ground, because newcomers avoid, or are driven off by, established pairs. This spacing out of breeding pairs would reduce the risk of starvation whether the birds collected their food inside their territories or not. Drs H. N. Kluijver and L. Tinbergen found evidence of this effect on great tits in the Netherlands, where the breeding population in broad-leaved woods remained almost constant from year to year while that of neighbouring coniferous woods, which are poorer in food resources, fluctuated widely;[17] and in England J. R.

Krebs found that when territorial great tits were removed from a wood others moved in from hedgerows to fill the vacancies.[18] This would suggest that territorial behaviour does limit the population of favourable habitats. However, population levels can rise suddenly and dramatically, even in rich broad-leaved woodland. In an oakwood section of the Forest of Dean, Gloucestershire, the average number of breeding pairs of great tits for 19 of the 20 years from 1945 to 1964 was 27, with a maximum of 45, but in 1957 the total rose to 75;[19] and in Marley Wood 86 pairs of great tits bred in 1961, although the maximum for the previous 14 years was 51 pairs.[20] In both these cases the woods were liberally provided with nest-boxes.

Other advantages from the defence of a breeding territory have been suggested, including strengthening of the pair bond, reducing the danger from mammalian predators and minimising the risk of epidemic disease, but conclusive proof of these effects on tit species in natural conditions is still lacking.

PAIR BOND AND NEST-SITE SELECTION

Few valid generalisations can be made about the pairing behaviour of the *Parus* genus. As mentioned above, many great and blue tits form pairs gradually within the winter flock before establishing a territory, but some male blue and great tits claim a nest-hole first and a mate later, and some coal tits acquire territories before mates. Some great, blue, coal and willow tits remain paired, with varying degrees of contact through the winter, while marsh and crested tits maintain a close association all the year round. The development of a new pair bond among great or blue tits in early spring is slow and gradual, but a bereaved marsh tit with a territory may obtain a new mate at any time of year without preliminaries. Averil Morley describes how birds that have lost mates suddenly acquire a replacement and the new partner immediately shows all the confidence of an established territory owner and uses the characteristic *pitchou* call.[21] Thereafter it is a case of 'till death us do part'; the pair are constantly together at all seasons and the distress of a bird that temporarily loses contact with its mate is obvious. Some juvenile marsh tits apparently pair off and acquire

Page 51 (*above*) A coal tit shows clearly its white nape, double wing bar and fine
bill; (*below*) a crested tit

Page 52 (*left*) A female great spotted woodpecker; (*right*) a nest-box photographed in Cumbria in 1972, showing woodpecker damage

territories in autumn but most of them spend the winter in a mixed flock and form pairs in the spring.

The persistence of a pair bond throughout the year in the more gregarious species may easily be overlooked, but the blue tit will demonstrate it in the attractive 'good-night' ceremony which is irregularly practised in early winter and spring. There are many variations in detail but as a rule the pair meet near the female's roost-hole and take a short flight together or indulge in a chase. If the female has entered the hole before the male arrives she will often emerge when he looks in and join him for a flight. When she finally settles for the night the male perches nearby and preens for a few minutes before retiring to his own roost, usually close at hand. The ceremony is generally simpler and less common in great tits, but the most elaborate performance I have seen was by a pair of coal tits on 2 March. This lasted 22 minutes, and it was 18 minutes after local sunset when the presumed female settled for the second and last time in her crevice in a walnut tree, after the pair had carried out a long series of complex swooping flights and pursuits with bursts of excited song.

A normally aggressive male may also show his recognition of his mate by allowing her to feed with him on a garden nut basket. Some pairs of great and coal tits will keep company through the winter, and a pair or, curiously, a trio of blue tits may also associate together and may indulge in courtship pursuits on mild days. The persistence of pairs is much more noticeable in a mild winter than in a severe one. It is the general rule for great tits to re-mate with their former partners each spring if both survive. Blue tits also remain faithful to the previous year's mate more often than not, but changes of partner during the lifetime of a former mate are less uncommon than in great tits. In the case of pairs that have separated for the winter it may be the link with the former territory or nest-hole rather than marital fidelity that is responsible for the re-mating.

R. A. Hinde found that the first stage of pair formation among great tits in the winter flocks was an attack by males, characterised by a short glide with spread tail and wings slightly open on alighting, on other great tits. Another male or unready female would respond with an aggressive posture or would flee, while a ready female would avoid the attack but usually stayed near by. Sudden attacks or 'pounces' and chases form an important part of the pre-breeding behaviour of all the tits, the male usually but not invariably being the aggressor. In early spring blue tits sometimes fly vertically up and then down with spread tails, and long-tailed tits perform a soaring flight followed by a steep descent with expanded tail.[22]

The blue tit often exhibits another form of flight display, practically restricted to the vicinity of the prospective nest-hole, a downward glide or a slow level flight with quick, short, moth-like beats of the widely spread wings. The moth-flight and glide are used most commonly by the male when returning to the nest tree. When the flight is performed in bright sunshine the misty blue effect of the rapidly vibrating wings is strikingly beautiful. It is most frequent in March and early April and is sometimes used as part of a threat to intruding tits, or even humans. It is only occasionally performed by great, coal and marsh tits, and then in a less developed form. R. A. Hinde has seen this flight used by a long-tailed tit, but these other species lack the wing colouring that gives the blue tit's display its special visual effectiveness.

The moth flight or glide by the male blue tit sometimes culminates in another form of display near the selected nest-hole or box. He perches with the body horizontal, the bend of the wing raised and wing-tips drooped, the tail partly raised and fanned and the nape feathers ruffled. Then with erect legs he hops rapidly towards the hole or nest-box, pivoting from side to side. He may then fly back and repeat the approach in the same way. A. W. Stokes called this display the 'dance'.[23] Other tit species adopt several of these postures without the movement towards the nest-hole.

Both these forms of courtship display by the blue tit, the moth flight or glide and the dance, are closely associated with the nest site. The process of choosing the site plays an important part in confirming the bond between the pair. In the earlier stages of courtship it is usual for great, blue and marsh tits to visit several possible holes. The male will fly to a nest-box or other likely hole, look in and then slowly turn his head from side to side, showing his conspicuous white cheeks. At other times he pecks repeatedly at the rim of the hole, and this activity should probably be regarded as a form of display rather than an attempt to enlarge the hole. Females also peck at nest-holes, and the female marsh tit is usually more active in this occupation than the male, who provides a vocal accompaniment of song and *pitchou* calls. Natural holes in trees, including some too small for any tit to enter, often have the surrounding bark completely chipped away. Both blue and great tits also do a good deal of hammering inside nest-boxes. This might be a rudimentary form of the excavation practised by willow tits and some crested tits, but it could also serve as a form of auditory display.

If the pairing takes place in February or early March, some days often elapse after the first inspection of a nest-hole before the male great or blue tit actually enters it, and perhaps another two or three weeks before the female follows. Even after a definite selection seems to have been made the pair may continue to visit other possible nest-holes. Great and blue tits often begin building in two or three different boxes before settling in one of them, and marsh and coal tits have been seen to do the same in natural holes. Indeed the final choice of nest site may be left very late. On 26 April 1968 ten nest-boxes were put up in a Lake District oak wood and five of them were occupied by blue tits, although by that date other blue tits in the district had already begun laying or had nearly finished building.

In most habitats coal tits have plenty of possible nest sites, and for a week or so in March and April the female spends much time investigating holes in the ground or in tree stumps. She may stay in a hole for one or two minutes and often brings out a piece of wood, moss or lichen. The male may ignore her activities, but sometimes he follows her closely and occasionally he searches for sites himself and displays over a likely hole with raised bill, fluttering wings and a trilling call. The commonest forms of courtship activity in coal tits are wing-fluttering and chasing, often noisier and more prolonged than in the other tits; but other forms of display have been observed, including a posture with fluffed body plumage and extended shivering wings accompanied by a 'curious, high-pitched whirring song'.[24]

Both male and female willow tits work at excavating a nest hole and this co-operation may help to strengthen the pair bond. Singing, bowing and chasing by the male and wing-shivering by both birds have been recorded.[7] The male crested tit has been described as fluttering round the tree-tops with persistent trilling,[25] and courtship chases are seen, as in other *Parus* species.

The so-called 'courtship feeding' and pre-copulatory actions of each species are closely associated with egg-laying and will be described in the next chapter.

4 The Nest and Eggs

THE NEST SITE

All the *Parus* tits normally nest in a hole of some kind. The hole may be a cavity in a tree, the ground, a wall, a box or some other human construction, each species showing a general preference for particular kinds of site. The most important requirement for all species seems to be a dark situation for the nest itself: if a nest is experimentally opened up, the parents will usually try to exclude the light by building up its side.

In choice of nest site, as in many other aspects of behaviour, blue tits are the most adaptable and least specialised of the tits. Nest-boxes and holes in trees and walls seem equally acceptable, and they may use old nests of other birds and even build in well-hidden forks of branches and trunks of trees. Indeed blue tits rival robins and wrens in the oddity of some of their nest sites: drainpipes, letterboxes, lamp-posts, inverted plant-pots, discarded petrol cans and many other unexpected artefacts, some of which have serious disadvantages for them. For example the iron gate or fence posts that they regularly use in some places become so hot in June sunshine that the nestlings can be seen panting in obvious distress. Two pairs of blue tits have been found occupying the 'top floor' of a beehive at the same time: they entered by the ventilation hole at the back and were separated from the bees by a layer of felt. In the absence of nest-boxes great tits are almost as catholic as blue tits in their choice of nest sites, and have been recorded building open nests in trees as well as using a variety of man-made cavities.

But tits will not be satisfied with any kind of hole. Those that use a ready-made one generally prefer it to have the smallest entrance they can squeeze through. This minimises danger from predators and also helps to reduce interspecific competition for nest sites, as many of the entrances used by blue and marsh tits are too small for great tits and tree sparrows. The species also differ in the height above ground and the type of site that they prefer.

The following table of 'natural' nest sites (ie excluding nest-boxes) used in a well-wooded area on the southern border of the English Lake District provides a fair comparison of the site preferences of four tit species under the same conditions. Most of the nests were found by following the flight of birds feeding young, and this should reduce any bias in favour of expected or accessible sites, although it may favour the recording of nests in open situations compared with those in dense woodland.

TABLE 3   NATURAL AND STONE WALL NEST SITES IN
NW ENGLAND

	Blue tit	Great tit	Coal tit	Marsh tit
Number of nests	120	70	35	25
Number over 3 metres above ground	30 (25%)	9 (13%)	0	0
Mean height*	2·3m	1·6m	0·4m	0·7m
Holes in ground	1 (1%)	4 (6%)	11 (31%)	3 (12%)
Retaining walls	11 (9%)	6 (9%)	16 (46%)	4 (16%)
Other walls	66 (55%)	26 (37%)	4 (11%)	3 (12%)
Holes in trees	31 (26%)	25 (36%)	4 (11%)	14 (56%)
Miscellaneous	11 (9%)	9 (13%)	0	1 (4%)

* Taking retaining walls as ground level.

A similar order of height preference has been shown with nest-boxes fixed at different levels, but there are of course exceptions. The highest nest in the above sample was a great tit's, over 10 metres up in the stone wall of a ruined tower; a blue tit was nesting at the same time only 2 metres from the ground in the same building. The table shows the strong liking of coal tits for retaining walls compared with the more plentiful walls of buildings, fields and roadsides. In the hilly district covered by this survey, roadside banks and garden terraces are often built up with dry (unmortared) stone walls, and the crevices

in these are in effect holes in an earth bank. The habit of nesting under-
ground appears to be innate in coal tits, not as has been suggested the
result of exclusion from tree holes by stronger species. Blue tits on
the other hand prefer holes in the walls of houses or farm buildings.
Marsh tits like tree holes, but in this district they sometimes nest in
walls and rock crevices even when apparently suitable tree holes are
available.

In their preferred British habitat of conifer plantations coal tits
usually nest in the stumps of felled trees, under their roots or under
rocks. The commonest site for crested tits is a rotten pine or birch
trunk or stump, but nests are also built in tiny cavities under the bark
of a living tree and sometimes in birch or alder stumps or fence posts.
Nests have been found from ground level to 13·7 metres above it:
the average of 32 nests reported in the Nest Record scheme of the
British Trust for Ornithology was just over 2 metres above ground.[1]

The essential requirement for willow tits is rotten wood that can
be excavated, favourite sites being dead trunks and branches of birch,
willow, alder and elder. On a south Lancashire peat moss, H. D. May
found that only birch trunks with a diameter of about 30cm were
used, but thinner trunks and branches are frequently excavated elsewhere.[2] Eighty-five Nest Record cards showed an average height
above ground of approximately 1 metre with only 2 nests over 3 metres,
but these figures may overestimate the proportion of low accessible
nests.

In spite of these differences there is still much competition for holes
in commercially managed woodland. This is shown by the marked
increase in the populations of tits and pied flycatchers in both broad-
leaved and coniferous woods when nest-boxes are provided. In
Czechoslovakia, Tichy claimed that the population of hole-nesting
birds could be increased almost fourfold in this way.[3] Even where
there are surplus boxes there may be interspecific competition for
some of them. Bruce Campbell relates a remarkable incident in the
Forest of Dean in which a redstart laid six eggs and a great tit eleven in
the same box, and the great tits fledged seven of their own young and
five redstarts.[4] Great tit and blue tit eggs in the same box occur every
year in the Lake District. Usually the great tits take over the box, put
a layer of nest material over the blue tits' eggs and hatch only their

own, but mixed great and blue tit broods have been fledged. Great tits generally dominate other hole-nesting species and sometimes kill a pied flycatcher in a box, but I have known six instances of pied flycatchers evicting great tits. In one of these cases, when the young flycatchers had flown great tits built a new nest, the top one of three, and laid a late clutch of eggs. Blue tits have also been known to evict great tits from a box.

Nearly all great tits and many blue tits prefer nest-boxes to natural holes. With the other species the reverse is generally the case, but there are wide regional differences in the use of boxes by coal tits and marsh tits, probably chiefly due to local variations in the number and suit-ability of natural holes, though a spread of the box-nesting habit by experience or imitation is also possible. Of 1,146 nests recorded over five years in boxes in woods in Cumbria and north Lancashire, chiefly broad-leaved but including some conifer plantations, only 4 were of coal tits and 9 of marsh tits, compared with 463 of great tits and 386 of blue tits. (The other box-occupants were nearly all pied flycatchers.) But in Thetford Forest in Norfolk and some other conifer plantations, the majority of coal tits occupy nest-boxes, if they are provided. Willow tits and Scottish crested tits are generally reluctant to nest in boxes, although willow tits have been induced to do so by the insertion in the box of some soft material like expanded polystyrene which they can excavate.

Excavation of a nest-hole is a habit developed to varying degrees in the different *Parus* species. All of them will remove odd chips of wood from inside the hole. Both great and marsh tits have been known, exceptionally, to excavate complete nest-sites in rotten wood, and a blue tit has been seen to enlarge a cavity to three times its original size.[5] I have also seen a blue tit carry fourteen beakfuls of mortar in quick succession out of a hole in a wall. But crested and willow tits are the regular diggers. Most of the nest-holes of crested tits are at least partly excavated, but hard wood is not removed and the final hole is often irregular in shape both internally and at the entrance. The female of a pair watched by Miss W. M. Ross did all the work, carrying off the last chip of wood after each short spell of digging; she completed the hole in five days.[6] Willow tits are more expert operators and excavate a miniature version of a woodpecker's hole.

The neatly shaped entrance is usually 4–5cm in diameter, and the hole then turns down along the branch or trunk to a depth of 15–30cm. Male and female usually share the task. Excavation may begin in the middle of March, but the early holes take three or four weeks to complete. Different pairs show varying diligence over the removal of chippings: some birds have been seen to carry away nearly all the excavated material, but more often they fly off with only the larger pieces, which are regularly dropped in the same place some 5 or 10 metres away. A litter of wood chips is often visible under a recently excavated hole.

NEST-BUILDING

In all the *Parus* tits the female is the nest-builder. The male often accompanies her on her visits to the nest-hole and sometimes enters it after her, but it is unusual for him to take an active part in building. Stuart Smith saw a male crested tit carry nest material into a hole at a late nest, and male blue tits have occasionally been recorded carrying material, but these incidents are exceptional. It is also normally the female who cleans the nest-box or cavity in preparation for building, though I have seen a male blue tit carry faeces out of a box in which he had been roosting before his mate began to build in it. Sometimes a considerable quantity of material is removed—one female blue tit took out over twenty loads in half an hour in mid-February—but often an old nest is left apparently intact and a new one built on top of it. The task of building the long-tailed tit's beautiful domed nest is shared between the male and female.

The date when building begins is much influenced by the weather. In Wytham Woods, near Oxford, great tits' nests were begun in the third week of April in 1947 but in the third week of March in 1948.[7] The rate of progress also depends on the weather. A cold or wet spell may stop building for several days, or even weeks, but then a few warm dry days will produce an outburst of building activity. The day's work usually reaches a peak in the late morning and wanes rapidly in the afternoon. Late nests, usually replacements for lost clutches, are often hurriedly and shoddily built, with little material and no proper lining; sometimes eggs are laid on bare wood surrounded by a ring of moss. The period from the bringing in of the first strands of nest material to the laying of the first egg averaged 18 days for 7 great tit nests in Westmorland begun in April (maximum 28 days, for one begun on 3 April), and 7 days for 12 nests begun between 1 and 11 May (minimum 4 days). Twelve blue tit nests begun in April averaged 16 days (maximum 30 days, for one begun on 4 April); 3 begun in May averaged 9 days. Dr and Mrs Lack found that first nests of long-tailed tits took from 17 to 25 days to complete, but replacement nests only 8–10 days.[8]

The nests of all the *Parus* tits are rather deep cups made of a wide variety of materials with good heat-insulation properties, the exact selection depending on local availability and individual choice. Moss is usually a major ingredient, except for the willow tit, which makes a more lightly constructed pad of vegetable fibres and fur. The great tit's nest, which may be taken as typical of those of the genus as a whole, normally has a foundation of loose moss and bents, and in it is shaped a cup of moss felted with wool, hair, fur or dead grasses. Moss fills up any superfluous space in the nesting cavity. But for two successive years a great tit began her nest in one of my boxes with a mass of dry roots while all her neighbours were using moss, and at a later stage the choice of lining may be equally individual. In Lake District woods the nests are usually lined with wool or with moss felted with deer hair, but occasionally a bird uses cow hair or other materials which must have been collected several hundred metres away. Some females show a preference for bright colours. One of my garden nests had a striking lining of red carpet material, of unknown origin, which made a most attractive contrast with the green moss surrounding it, and I have found a proportion of red wool in the lining of two other nests over a kilometre from the nearest house. A Cumberland bird with sombre tastes lined her nest with black wool and black feathers.[9]

Blue tits nesting in boxes are more likely to start by filling in the corners, and the lining usually includes more feathers, grass and vegetable fibres. Both great and blue tits often build up a wall of material under the entrance hole and usually construct the cup of the nest against the back wall. Blue tits may rob other species for nest material: I have known them dismantle completely two chaffinches' nests, and blue tits have been seen taking rabbit fur out of a willow tit's nest-hole and wool or hair out of crows' nests. A marsh tit's nest is very much like a small great tit's, with moss the basic material; a coal tit's is again similar but is generally less bulky and is lined with fur, hair or lichen. Crested tits' nests are generally rather slightly built, with a foundation of dead moss and a lining of deer hair, hare fur, vegetable down and sometimes feathers.

The nest of the long-tailed tit is well known as the most elaborate architectural achievement of any British bird. It is in effect an oval bag of closely felted moss and lichen thickly lined with feathers and with a small opening near the top. It is placed in a wide range of situations, from an open fork 18 metres up in a tree to the end of a conifer branch or a low tangle of brambles, but in general low situations are preferred, especially in thorny bushes. Tree nests, in spite of their apparently effective camouflage, suffer heavier losses from predation. A pair of long-tailed tits may change from one kind of situation to an entirely different one for a replacement nest. Their building is done by a very limited range of pushing, pulling and weaving movements and by the rotation of the body, but their innate skill in the selection of the right materials, in the right proportions and at the right stage of construction, and in the shaping of the roof, is remarkable. The tiny pieces of lichen and moss are bonded together with spiders' webs to form a surprisingly strong and elastic felt, so that when a bird is working inside the whole nest can be seen in a state of violent convulsion without any rupture of the fabric. The final lining of feathers must represent hours of labour and travelling time; more than 2,000 feathers have been counted in some nests.

In some parts of eastern England and in large cities, the lichens which seem so essential a part of the outer covering of long-tailed tits' nests in most of Britain are virtually unobtainable. In 1974 paper, chiefly soft tissue, was used as a substitute in three out of four nests in Regents Park,[10] and elsewhere two nests have been found with large numbers of polystyrene chips woven into the moss.[11]

During the later stages of nest-building, two new forms of apparent courtship display are seen, 'courtship feeding' and wing-shivering. These are common to all the *Parus* species. Feeding of the female by the male may begin several days before the first egg is laid. At first the actions are quick, unobtrusive and unsolicited, and may in fact be only symbolic. I have seen male great and blue tits momentarily 'kiss' their mates at the entrance hole of the nest cavity, a fortnigh or more before the first egg was laid, without any visible exchange of food. When egg-laying begins, 'courtship feeding' tends to become more excited and emotional. The female usually takes up a 'begging baby' attitude, crouching low with shivering drooped wings and raised bill and tail and uttering calls that bear some resemblance to the hunger calls of fledglings. The male often shivers his wings and calls at the same time. Feeding becomes more frequent during egg-laying and increases again when incubation begins, but the male's feeding activity often dwindles towards the end of the incubation period. Sometimes he takes food into the nest-hole for the incubating female, but more often he calls her out and feeds her nearby.

It was formerly believed that the main, if not the only, function of 'courtship feeding' was to strengthen the bond between paired birds, the equivalent of the young man's gift of chocolates to his girl friend, but Dr T. Royama claimed that it serves a much more practical purpose.[12] A female great tit, for example, would have great difficulty in collecting sufficient food for herself during the egg-laying period to produce each day an egg weighing about 1·5gm, or enough to sustain herself during incubation when she can only leave the nest for short periods. Dr Royama estimated that a female great tit received about 60 feeds a day from her mate during the egg-laying period and about 150 a day during incubation, female blue tits receiving an average of 60 feeds in 100 minutes. This food service could well be essential for successful breeding, a theory supported by the facts that it is much commoner during incubation than in the pre-coition period, and that it is more frequent in the blue tit than in the great tit, which provides larger food items. Even before egg-laying begins, female tits may need extra food to compensate for their expenditure of time and energy in nest-building.

Nevertheless, some link between this kind of feeding and courtship is suggested by the fact that the food-begging posture of the female closely resembles that of sexual invitation. When soliciting coition the female great tit crouches low, with head and tail raised, shivers her wings, and calls. The male also often crouches with head drawn back and shivers his wings with repeated *zeedle* or *zee* calls. This preliminary display is usually continued for several seconds before the male mounts.

Actions of this kind seem to be common to all the tits, although each incident differs in detail. Averil Morley described the male marsh tit 'floating down' on to his mate with a 'low *yu-yu-yu* song-note of a beautiful and tender quality'. Stuart Smith wrote that the male crested tit 'flutters around with raised crest, continuously calling with the characteristic spluttering trill. The female answers with a lower-pitched, quieter trill.' Sometimes the male initiates the act, sometimes he responds to invitation by the female—though occasionally he attacks her instead. Coition usually begins four or five days before the first egg is laid and occurs most frequently in the early morning. Great and marsh tits usually mate in bushes or on low branches, but pairs of blue and coal tits may copulate in the tree tops well over 15 metres above the ground. After coition both male and female continue wing-shivering for a few seconds, and the male sometimes feeds his mate immediately afterwards.

THE EGGS

The eggs of the titmice are very much alike in appearance. All have a whitish ground colour, but when fresh the yolk shows through the thin shells with a delicate pink flush. They are normally spotted with reddish-brown, but completely white eggs are not uncommon, and in all species the extent of the spotting and blotching varies. Great tits' eggs are generally noticeably larger than the other species', but as their weight, excluding freak specimens, ranges from 1·40 to 2·10gm, and blue tits' may weigh up to 1·25gm, occasional errors in identification even by experienced nest-box recorders are understandable. Crested tits' eggs are particularly strongly marked, but even an expert oologist might have difficulty in identifying the others without seeing the nest or a parent bird. When the first egg has been laid one is usually added each day until the clutch is complete, but, at least in great and blue tits' nests, a gap of a day sometimes occurs in the laying of the series. Exceptionally, two eggs may be laid on the same day. The hen usually lays early in the morning before leaving the nest for the first time.

A curious habit common to all the *Parus* species is that of covering over the eggs during the period before incubation begins. Many great and blue tits conceal their eggs in nest-boxes so effectively that there is no sign of them or the cup that holds them, and inexperienced observers might conclude that the nest was still under construction. The bird brings in fresh material each morning and lays it loosely over the eggs, later weaving it into the nest. Crested tits cover their eggs completely,[13] and in two willow tit nests observed through artificial windows the eggs were also deeply covered. Yet sometimes the covering by great, blue and coal tits is only superficial, or non-existent. The function of this behaviour is not obvious. Protection from the cold seems unnecessary in a well-insulated nest inside a hole, and there is no indication of better covering in cold weather. In the exceptionally warm May of 1970, I found 5 out of 31 incomplete great tit clutches uncovered, and 2 out of 18 blue tits'; in the very cold May of 1972, 7 out of 27 great tit clutches, and 5 out of 12 blue tits' were uncovered. A clutch might be left bare one day and covered the next. Concealment from intruding predators, such as young humans, is a possible advantage.

In *The Natural Regulation of Animal Numbers*, Dr Lack proposed that the breeding season of birds was adjusted to provide the maximum supply of food for the young, quoting as an example the apparent fact that the nestling period of tits coincides with a glut of caterpillars in the oakwoods which are the favoured habitat of great, blue and marsh tits. Subsequently Dr Perrins has shown that young great tits from the earliest broods in broad-leaved woodland have a much better chance of survival than those from later ones, and he concludes that earlier breeding would benefit the species.[14] However, egg-laying appears to be delayed by the inability of the female to obtain enough food to form eggs sooner. A great tit's full clutch of eggs weighs about as much as the female herself, and a blue tit's may amount to 150 per cent of the mother's weight, so even with the help of 'court-ship feeding' a good supply of nutritious food for the female is critical for the precise timing of egg-laying. Nevertheless, although the time of greatest need of the young may thus not coincide exactly with the maximum supply of food, there is a fair approximation to it for the great tit and a slightly better one for blue and marsh tits.

The British tit species show small but generally consistent differences in the time of peak egg-laying activity, although there is much overlapping by individual pairs. The long-tailed tit breeds considerably earlier than any of the *Parus* tits. Near Oxford the mean date of the first egg over a period of six years was nineteen days earlier than that for great tits, but only a few days separate the egg-laying peaks of the other species. The following table of first-egg dates is derived from the Nest Record Cards of the British Trust for Ornithology.

TABLE 4   DATE OF FIRST EGG OF 4 *PARUS* SPECIES

Species	Region	Years	Number of clutches	Mean date
Coal tit	England and Wales	1965–70	86	29 April
	N Scotland	1965–70	30	28 April
Crested tit	N Scotland	1950–71	7	23 April
Marsh tit	England and Wales	1962–71	70	28 April
Willow tit	England and Wales	1948–71	26	1 May

Notes:
1 First eggs laid after 10 May are excluded as these may represent second broods or replacement clutches.
2 The comparatively late date for coal tits in England is due to a number of records from conifer plantations over 150 metres above sea level in Lancashire and Yorkshire, where laying was consistently several days later than in plantations near sea level by the Moray Firth. Most of the crested tit records also come from the latter area: nests 240 metres higher in the Spey valley are generally some days later.
3 The validity of the date for the willow tit is uncertain because of the wide range of laying dates each year, often due to abandoned excavations or evictions.

Blue tits generally begin laying 3 or 4 days later than coal or marsh tits, and great tits on average 1 or 2 days later than blue tits. It is difficult to account for the early breeding of crested and coal tits, the two species with a preference for conifers, considering that great, blue and coal tits are more successful in rearing young in late broods than in early ones in pine plantations.

It should be emphasised that the first-egg dates shown above are averages over a period of several years. In practice the egg-laying peak of each species may vary by as much as a month from one year to another according to weather conditions, and the actual date on which a particular female tit lays her first egg in a given year is affected by a number of complex factors. Experiments have shown that in north temperate latitudes the breeding season of several species of

The Nest and Eggs

birds, including the great tit, is partly controlled by the increasing day-length in spring, irrespective of temperature; but both in Holland and near Oxford the egg-laying dates of great tits have also been found to be closely correlated with the temperature throughout March and April. In addition to this long-term effect of temperature there is often a more immediate response, with a time-lag of only about four days, to a spell of warm weather between late March and early May. If this follows a period of cold weather, as happened in the first week of May 1970, egg-laying begins simultaneously in many nests, even of different species of tits.

Regional differences in breeding dates within the British Isles may also be due to variations of temperature, probably through their effect upon food supply. Great and blue tits in southern England begin to lay a week or more earlier than those in the north and up to 2½ weeks earlier than those in Scotland: in Marley Wood, near Oxford, between 1955 and 1964, the mean date of great tits' first eggs varied from 17 April to 5 May, and of blue tits' from 15 April to 4 May. Mean clutch sizes ranged from 8·0 to 10·0 for great tits, and from 8·5 to 11·3 for blue tits.

Altitude as well as latitude influences the date of egg-laying. For example, in 1969 great tits' first eggs in nests 213–366m (700–1200ft) above sea level in the Lake District averaged 17 May, those under 91m (300ft) 11 May. The corresponding figures for blue tits were 15 and 10 May. But in 1970, with the sudden burst of warm weather in the first week of May after a cold wet April, the mean date, 10 May, was the same for both species in both high and low woodlands. Pied flycatchers varied in parallel with the tits in both years.

The date of egg-laying is also influenced to some extent by habitat. Great tits begin laying on average a few days earlier in gardens than in woods, and earlier in Scots pine than in Corsican pine plantations. There may also be regular differences of a few days between great tits' breeding dates in different woods of apparently similar composition in the same district. They are probably due to variations in the food supply available to the female tits for the formation of eggs, which may depend, in broad-leaved woodland, upon the time of the opening of the leaf buds. The presence of early leaved trees like syca-mores, with their often numerous aphids, might enable tits to breed

68

earlier. P. J. Jones has produced evidence that animal food is required for the formation of eggs, for breeding is not earlier in springs with abundant remaining stocks of winter seed food, but woodland great tits in Sweden provided with trays of mealworms in spring began to lay three to six days earlier than those without extra food.[15]

The first-egg date for great tits is influenced not only by these environmental factors—length of daylight, temperature in the long and short term, geographical latitude, altitude and habitat—but also by differences in the birds themselves. Kluijver, Perrins and others have found that one-year-old females usually lay a few days later than older birds, and females two or more years old tend to lay at similar dates in successive years. Consequently the average date of the first egg in a given area for a particular year will be affected by the proportion of first-year females in the population, as well as by weather conditions. Small females also lay earlier than large ones.

CLUTCH SIZE

The tits in general lay more eggs than most passerine birds, and the blue tit produces a larger clutch than any other nidicolous species. Blue tit nests near Oxford had an average of over 13 eggs in two successive years and included clutches of 18 and 19; great tits' clutches averaged between 9 and 10 eggs. However British tits do not often produce second broods, so that a blackbird laying three clutches of 4 or 5 eggs in a season may exceed their annual total. Table 5 shows the clutch sizes of the other British *Parus* tits as indicated by the Nest Record Cards of the British Trust for Ornithology.

TABLE 5 CLUTCH SIZES OF FIRST BROODS OF 4 *PARUS* SPECIES IN BRITAIN

Species	Region	Years	No of clutches	Max	Min	Mean
Coal tit	England and Wales	1965–70	114	13	6	9·4
	Scotland	1965–70	32	11	6	8·4
Crested tit	N Scotland	1950–71	21	6	4	5·2
Marsh tit	England and Wales	1962–71	95	10	4	7·7
Willow tit	England and Wales	1948–71	42	13	4	7·4

E

The clutch sizes of the tit species may be related to the size of the nest cavity: the comparatively small clutches of crested and willow tits would suit their constricted excavated holes. The large clutches often laid by blue and great tits in nest-boxes could be partly a response to the generous floor space usually available in a box, but the wide range of clutch sizes found in identical boxes shows that other factors must also be involved. It is difficult to count the eggs in a long-tailed tit's nest without causing it serious damage, but from the available data the average clutch in Britain appears to be 9 or 10.

One factor favouring the laying of large clutches of eggs by birds that nest in holes is the comparative security of the nestlings. Young birds in an open nest are extremely vulnerable to predation, so it is to the advantage of such species to use the available food to raise a small brood in a short time, while the *Parus* tits can afford to feed a larger brood of nestlings over a longer period in comparative safety. It is more difficult to explain the large average clutches of long-tailed tits, whose nests are often destroyed by jays, magpies and other predators. However, the domed nest does provide some concealment, and predation is less damaging in the nestling period, when the leaves of deciduous trees are providing cover, than during egg-laying and incubation.

The number of eggs in the clutches laid by tits, particularly great tits, has been the subject of much detailed study both on the continent and in Britain as part of a programme of research into factors which might affect the regulation of populations of these species. Each nidicolous species may have evolved through natural selection a clutch size—to quote Dr Lack—'to correspond with that brood size from which, on average, most surviving young are produced, the limit normally being set by the amount of food that the parents can collect for their nestlings'. Any hereditary tendency to lay oversize or undersize clutches would be eliminated, because comparatively few young would survive from such broods; and in fact great tit clutches of average size, 9 or 10 eggs, near Oxford have been found in most years to produce most surviving young. But for the tit family this general principle has not resulted in the evolution of a specific clutch size which is closely adhered to, as is the case with some sea-birds, pigeons and other genera. On the contrary the tits produce a very wide range of clutch sizes. For instance I have found complete great tit clutches begun in the same week of the same year in the same wood varying from 3 to 10 eggs, and blue tit clutches in similar conditions ranging from 5 to 16.

These variations, like those in breeding dates, can be partly explained by differences between individual birds. One-year-old female great tits generally lay smaller clutches than older birds, and each older female tends to lay a similar number of eggs in successive years, though this is subject to variation according to external circumstances. C. M. Perrins has also detected a hereditary tendency for daughter great tits to lay clutches similar to their mothers'. But there are also more general factors affecting average clutch size. In a species like the great tit with a wide geographical range, there are marked regional differences. The number of eggs in the clutch of many birds in the northern hemisphere tends to increase with distance from the tropics, and in general the great tit follows this trend, with an average clutch of 3 in India, 7–9 in Spain and over 10 in southern England. These differences are probably an adaptation to climatic conditions. If the air temperature is high, feathered nestlings in a large brood suffer distress and may risk death from hyperthermia, while in cold conditions a small brood of recently hatched young cannot maintain the necessary body heat. On the other hand the general trend towards larger clutches in the north seems to be reversed in the British Isles, where great, blue and coal tits lay larger clutches, and more often produce second broods, in the south of England than in northern England and in Scotland (see Tables 5 and 6). Possible reasons for this are discussed below.

There are also considerable differences in clutch size related to habitat. Great and blue tits lay fewer eggs in gardens and in Corsican pine plantations than in broad-leaved woods, and Table 6 shows that great tit nests in mixed broad-leaved woods in the Lune valley average 2 eggs more than those in limestone woods dominated by yew, ash and sycamore 25km away.

Clutch sizes are also affected by the date when the eggs are laid. Late clutches, whether delayed first attempts, replacements or genuine second broods, are nearly always well below average size. Near Oxford, clutches tended to be lower in years when breeding for all pairs was delayed by unfavourable weather, and to be lower in woods in which egg-laying was later than normal for the district. Yet in

Cumbria in 1970, a late breeding year, great tit clutches were well up to average; and nests in limestone woods are usually early but have small clutches.

TABLE 6   AVERAGE CLUTCH SIZE OF GREAT AND BLUE TITS IN CUMBRIA AND N LANCASHIRE

Year	Lake District (oaks)		Limestone (yew, ash, etc)		Lune valley	
	great	blue	great	blue	great	blue
1968	7·1	9·7	6·5	8·6	9·0	9·5
1969	7·7	9·1	6·2	(11·0)*	9·2	9·6
1970	8·3	9·3	7·2	8·6	9·5	10·5
1971	8·2	10·1	6·8	(6·7)*	8·1	8·4
1972	7·2	9·0	6·4	7·2	8·8	9·5
1973	7·2	9·7	6·7	9·1	8·6	9·6
Mean	7·6	9·5	6·6	8·4	8·9	9·5

* Based on less than 5 nests, so excluded from 'Mean'.

A discovery of great interest in connection with the regulation of bird populations was made in the Netherlands by Dr H. N. Kluijver, who found that when the numbers of great tits in a wood increased, second broods were less common and first clutches tended to be smaller than normal. This 'density-dependent' clutch size has also been demonstrated in woods near Oxford for great tits and blue tits, and in Breckland conifer plantations for coal tits. In view of the very heavy mortality of young tits after they leave the nest, it might appear that these minor adjustments in the numbers of eggs laid would have no effect upon the number of tits surviving to breed in the following year, but J. R. Krebs has calculated that they do appreciably affect local populations of great tits.[16]

At first sight the factors affecting clutch size may appear to resemble those controlling the date of egg-laying. Both are influenced by regional differences, by type of habitat and by the age of the female parent. However, the sufficiency of food for the female to form eggs, which seems so vital in determining the date of laying the first egg, cannot be a major influence in deciding the size of the clutch, for larger clutches are laid early in the season when food is scarce than later when it is plentiful. Moreover, females can lay replacement clutches almost immediately after the loss of first ones. In fact it appears that the size of clutch laid by tits is adapted not to the supply of food for the adult female but to the quantity that will be available for the nestlings three or four weeks after the eggs are laid. Thus the smaller clutches in northern Britain may be due to a less abundant supply of insect larvae in northern woods in late May and early June. Though it would be difficult accurately to compare the quantities of food available for nestlings in northern and southern regions of Britain, the ravages of defoliating caterpillars on oak trees are noticeably less severe in the north. It may be that higher summer temperatures in the south produce a heavier crop of insects, and the effects of rainfall may also be involved; Bruce Campbell has suggested that heavy rain may wash invertebrate food off the trees. It is also likely that both adult tits and nestlings need more food to maintain their body heat in wet weather, and it is known that the parents' nest-visiting frequency is restricted during heavy rain. It would be more difficult for tits to raise large broods in districts with a high rainfall, so that small clutches would have a special advantage in north-west England.

The relation of clutch size to habitat seems to depend on the food supply for nestlings: both great and blue tits lay more eggs among the mature broad-leaved trees which provide most invertebrate food for the young. The small clutch laid by a first-year female seems to be adapted to her inexperience in collecting food for a family—it is more productive for a pair of tits to raise a few well-fed fledglings than a large brood of underfed ones. Underweight young have a poor chance of survival.

The reduction of clutch size when population is dense could be achieved through the pressure of numbers on the adults at the time of egg-laying, for example by producing frequent territorial disputes. It would certainly not be surprising if overcrowding had a direct effect upon egg-production, but it is difficult to understand the mechanism by which tits can adjust their clutches to habitat conditions and breeding dates which will affect food supplies after the lapse of three or four weeks.

INCUBATION

In the tit family it is only the female who incubates the eggs. If the male enters the nest-hole it is normally to take food to his mate, though he may occasionally stay in for two or three minutes, and I once found a male (colour-ringed) blue tit brooding four eggs and four newly hatched young when the female had just left them.

The actual beginning of incubation is not as precise and clear-cut as was generally believed some years ago, when the Rev F. C. R. Jourdain stated categorically in *The Handbook of British Birds* that for the blue tit 'incubation begins with the last egg but two'. Great and blue tits generally begin their incubation gradually. For a day or two before the completion of the clutch the female may sit for some hours in the afternoon but not in the morning. This gradual start is also shown by the fact that the earlier eggs of a clutch hatch in any order but the last two or three hatch in the order in which they were laid. Dr Gibb found that the 'apparent start of incubation' (the day on which the female was first found sitting, or the eggs warm, during the day) varied from three days before the completion of the clutch to four days after. 'Apparent incubation' most commonly began with the penultimate egg in a late season and with the last egg in an early one. Blue tits showed similar trends but no instances were recorded of 'apparent incubation' beginning more than one day after the completion of the clutch. Incubation starts relatively earlier with late or second broods. A. Deadman records that coal tits do not begin to incubate before the completion of the clutch.[17]

Incubating females have quite frequent breaks in their brooding duties during daylight, but there is some individual variation in the length of the periods on and off the nest. An Oxford great tit alternated periods of about 25 minutes on the eggs with about 10 minutes off on the day before hatching. During the female's absence the maximum drop in temperature was $5.5°$ C, an indication of the effective heat insulation of the nest. Average periods off the nest of five to ten minutes have been recorded for blue, coal, marsh and willow tits. Absences tend to become shorter towards hatching time. A break in incubation by any species may begin when the male calls out his mate to receive food. After taking it she may return immediately to the nest, or may fly off, either alone or with her mate, for several minutes.

Even during the incubation period additions of material are made to the nest by great and blue tits. Sometimes these consist of bits of green leaf or fern frond—a kind of nest decoration usually associated with birds of prey. There are other indications that the nest-building drive of tits is not necessarily exhausted when incubation begins. In a series of experiments with great and blue tits' nests in boxes it was found that the adults would make alterations or repairs to their nests during incubation or even when they had feathered young.[18] When one side of the box was replaced with glass or a perforated metal sheet, the birds built up that side of the nest to darken the interior, and when part of the nest was cut away they rebuilt it, either with fresh material or with cotton wool provided by the experimenters.

The explosive hiss with which a sitting female *Parus* tit may greet an intruder is a striking feature of brooding behaviour. She appears to inflate her whole body, and at the same time raises her wings and expands her tail; then with a sort of thudding spit she expels the air with her bill wide open and smartly closes her wings. The whole process is then repeated. The great tit's performance is perhaps the most impressive, but brooding marsh and blue tits also produce a hiss that might scare off a predator. Willow tits sit closely but apparently rarely hiss. This form of deterrent seems to be most frequent shortly before and after the hatching of the eggs, and at this time some great tits can be heard hissing while one is still approaching the nest-box tree.

5 The Nestlings

The incubation period, the time from the beginning of 'apparent incubation' to the hatching of the eggs, varies appreciably from one pair to another, even within the same tit species. J. A. Gibb found that the incubation period of 55 great tits' clutches ranged from 12 to 15 days, and for blue tits from 13 to 16 days. The average period for great tits was 13·9 days and for blue tits 14·2. The hatching of a clutch of great or blue tit eggs was found to extend over a period of 1–5 days according to the stage at which incubation began: 101 out of 190 clutches hatched over a period of three days.[1] Some puzzling nest-box records suggest the possibility that incubation periods may occasionally be extended much beyond normal limits, perhaps because of delayed or intermittent sitting by the female.

A female will sometimes sit for a surprisingly long time on infertile eggs. A great tit in one of my boxes had 8 warm eggs on 10 May 1971 and was found sitting on several subsequent days up to and including 14 June, 35 days later. The eggs were found deserted on 23 June.

The incubation periods of the other tits are similar, and are generally given as between 13 and 15 days. A. Deadman records 10–14 days for the coal tit in Scotland.

The reactions of parents to the hatching of the eggs are varied. Some great and blue tits show considerable excitement, with both parents repeatedly going in and out of the box and the male immediately increasing his rate of food-carrying. Near the nesting-hole the male resumes at hatching time the wing-shivering that formerly served as a prelude to coition. Whether he discovers the hatching of the eggs by looking into the nesting-hole in the absence of his mate, or whether she communicates with him in some way is not clear. However, this decisive response to hatching is not an invariable rule. Of the marsh tits watched by Averil Morley, one male 'would scarcely leave the nest alone', but the other pairs did not alter their rhythm from that of the second half of the incubation period, and one male only visited the nest twice in 65 minutes on the day of hatching.

It is probably normal for the female to carry out the egg-shells immediately after hatching. Great, blue, coal, crested and long-tailed tits certainly do this sometimes, but great and marsh tits have been seen to eat the shells of newly hatched eggs and this may also happen with the other species. A blue tit has been observed to carry away an addled egg. As an egg is sometimes unaccounted for when the young have flown this action may be not uncommon among great and blue tits; small dead young may be removed in the same way. More often, however, infertile eggs and dead young are buried in the nest material or simply left in the cup of the nest.

During the hatching period and for a day or two afterwards the female continues to brood the young for the greater part of the day: this is probably essential while they are very small and naked. The male brings food to his mate on the nest and she receives it and passes it on to the nestlings. On the second day the female usually begins to bring food for the young, but up to the fourth day she broods them for about half the daylight hours. Then after the 11th day she no longer broods in daytime and stops roosting in the nest-hole soon afterwards. By the end of the first week after hatching the cock and hen are usually sharing the feeding on roughly equal terms, but the contribution of the sexes varies greatly at different nests. At one great tit nest the female's visits increased from about 50 per cent of the total on the 9th day to 91 per cent on the 19th.[2] Both sexes of coal, marsh, willow and long-tailed tits share feeding duties, and this may also be normal for crested tits, but at one nest the hen appeared to do all the feeding even from the first day,[3] and Deadman found that only one parent fed the broods of fledged young.[4]

For details of the behaviour of marsh, willow and crested tits after the hatching of the eggs we are still almost entirely dependent upon external observation, but the situation is different with the species that regularly nest in boxes. In recent times both professional and amateur ornithologists have used a variety of espionage techniques for observing and recording the domestic affairs of great, blue and coal tits. One of the earliest developments, and in some respects still the most useful, was the observation nest-box with a darkened window through which the observer could watch, at a few inches' range, everything that happened at the nest. An artificial gape, resembling the open mouth of a nestling, has been used in nests, or by the entrance hole, to collect samples of the food brought to the young. Electrical devices have been installed to register every entry into the nest-hole, and great tits have taken flashlight photographs of themselves and the prey they were carrying every time they entered the box.[5] But even the most sophisticated mechanical bird recorders have their limitations. For the last few days before the nestlings fly their parents almost invariably feed them at the entrance hole without entering the box, and a photograph would only reveal a rear view of a hungry nestling.

An observation box shows aspects of parental care that would otherwise be unknown. One curious feature of the feeding of the young, at least by great and blue tits, is the way in which an adult will place an item of food in one nestling's open mouth, then withdraw it and thrust it into another's. A female great tit often tries three or four different mouths before letting go of the food. N. D. Pullen, who watched blue tits do this, believed the adult was waiting for the nestling to close its mouth on the food and was thus selecting the hungriest chick.[6] This explanation is supported by the fact that to be successful an artificial gape has to simulate the grasping action as well as the appearance of a nestling's mouth.

Nest sanitation is especially important for hole-nesting species because of the enclosed space and the long fledging period. In all species of tits the faeces are usually swallowed by the parents for the first three or four days after hatching; after that the parents carry away the gelatinous faecal sacs and either drop them or wipe them off their bills on a twig. Both sexes share this task. The droppings are removed, one at a time, about once in five to ten visits, or very roughly once in every 100 minutes for each nestling, but the production of faeces tends to increase during the nestling period. On most visits to the nest the adult delivers the food and flies away after a quick look round, but sometimes it watches intently for several seconds and seizes a faecal sac as it emerges. After the first few days, when a nestling is about to defaecate it hoists itself up in the nest and stands with head down and raised posterior as though trying to touch its toes with its bill. A ring of white feathers round the cloaca makes a conspicuous target for the parents in the dim light of the nest-hole. Feathered long-tailed tit nestlings have been seen clinging to the roof of the nest with their tails towards the entrance hole; the parent then receives the faecal sac while perched just outside the nest. But the droppings are sometimes deposited by the nestlings at the side of the entrance hole. Nest sanitation is maintained by the *Parus* tits until the young fly, but long-tailed tits are not always so particular.

A habit found in many nidicolous species but especially highly developed in the tits is the prodding and pulling inflicted upon the nest while it is occupied by young. This is a very thorough and vigorous operation carried out chiefly, perhaps only, by the female. She digs and tugs at the lining and foundations for two or three minutes at a time and about once an hour, with little concern for the disturbance caused to the occupants. She can sometimes be seen nibbling something in her bill when she raises her head, but I know of no definite evidence that she is removing flea larvae or other parasites, as has been suggested. Her activity may maintain the heat-insulation properties of the nest until the young are well feathered: without being pulled about it would be trodden down into a thin flat pad much earlier. A possibly accidental by-product of the operation is the burial of addled eggs and dead nestlings.

Although the growth of the nestlings varies considerably with their food intake, the development of their plumage and the different stages of behaviour are independent of size, being closely linked with actual age. Day-to-day development seems to be similar in all the *Parus* species. J. A. Gibb found that in both great and blue tits secondary covert feathers and secondaries emerged on the 8th and 9th days, primaries and primary coverts on the 10th and 11th. On the 14th and 15th days the tips of the secondary coverts meet the base of the secondaries, and on the 15th and 16th days the tips of the primary coverts meet the base of the primaries. The expanded wing then has an unbroken surface and the bird can fly.

The eyes only begin to open about 9 days after hatching. Nestlings seem to be sensitive to light well before the eyes open, and they will gape in response to a dark shadow across the entrance hole as well as to sounds and small movements of the box. Their hunger calls are first audible from about the 9th day. They first show fear at about 10 or 12 days and will then cower down in the nest when approached or alarmed by a loud noise. From the 14th day they are liable to explode from the nest if disturbed, and an occasional brood of great tits may leave the nest at about that age for no apparent reason. The average fledging period for great and blue tits is 19 days, but in unfavourable conditions the young may stay in the nest over three weeks. The fledging period of the other *Parus* tits is rather shorter: the average for coal, marsh and willow tits is nearer 16 than 19 days. Bruce Campbell gives 18 days as the average for crested tits.

FEEDING THE YOUNG

The most vital of the parental duties of tits, as of other nidicolous birds, during the nestling period is of course the provision of food for the chicks. The relationship between brood size, food supply and survival of young great, blue and coal tits has been studied in various habitats by a succession of Oxford zoologists under the direction of David Lack. The highly compressed and simplified statement of fact and hypothesis in the next few pages is based chiefly on the published results of research by J. A. Gibb, Monica M. Betts and C. M. Perrins.

The feeding of nestling great and blue tits in an oak wood (Forest of Dean) was studied by Monica Betts. Information on the food items brought by the parents was obtained for a brood of great tits and a brood of blue tits in observation boxes. Although defoliating caterpillars formed a considerable proportion of the diet of both species, the two broods differed over the most favoured items. The following table shows the percentages of different kinds of food taken by the two broods between 13 and 18 June, when both were still in the nest.

Blue tits were experts in extracting pupae of tortricoid moths from rolled-up oak leaves, but only great tits fed adult insects to their young. Spiders and their eggs are so regularly given to nestling tits of all species, especially in their early life, that they may have some special nutritional value. Grit and crushed snails are also regular items in small quantities and presumably serve as an aid to digestion. Dr Betts noted that the great tits brought a load of this mixture on average twice a day and on each occasion shared it among half the brood, so that each nestling would normally receive a daily dose. The size of the food items brought to the great tit nest increased steadily during the nestling period, being mostly 4–12mm long before the 6th day and 15–24mm from the 16th to 20th days. The items brought to young blue tits at all ages were usually under 10mm long.

TABLE 7   FOOD OF GREAT AND BLUE TIT NESTLINGS IN OAK WOODLAND (BETTS, 1955)

	Great tit		Blue tit	
Age in days	15–17	18–20	7–9	10–12
Larvae of lepidoptera	66	42	58	27
Pupae of lepidoptera	12	17	23	61
Imagines of lepidoptera	6	32	0	0
Other insects	7	5	0	0
Spiders and egg cocoons	7	2	17	11
Other foods	2	2	2	1

Neither species was bringing in food simply in proportion to its local abundance. In the first week of June caterpillars of the winter moth *Operophtera brumata* made up 59 per cent of all defoliating larvae present in samples of leaves, but they formed less than 30 per cent of the food taken to the young great tits. In Dutch pine woods Dr L. Tinbergen found that great tits took relatively fewer caterpillars of the pine beauty moth *Panolis griseovariegata* when the latter were very abundant. The birds seem to like to provide a varied diet even at the cost of more searching. Great tits are particularly catholic and adaptable in their selection of food items. I watched one male systematically tear open a hanging wasps' nest and take all the larvae and pupae from it to his nestlings, and great tits have been seen to carry large caterpillars to the nest, bite their heads off and squeeze the contents of their bodies, like toothpaste out of a tube, into the expectant mouths of the nestlings. A long-tailed tit has been filmed feeding a nestling in the same way.

In the pine plantations of Thetford Chase, caterpillars made up about 50 per cent of the food of great, blue and coal tits, though the parents sometimes flew up to 400m to collect larvae from scattered broad-leaved trees for the nestlings of their first broods.[7] Caterpillars were particularly scarce in Corsican pines. In June and July prey became more abundant in the pines, and the tits fed later broods successfully from neighbouring trees. The proportions of the prey species differed widely from year to year. The diet of the great tit was the most varied and the items the largest. Blue tit nestlings in the pines received similar food to those in broad-leaved woods. Coal tits took many spiders, a few aphids and miscellaneous insects; their items were the smallest, although larger than the average of samples taken in the pines.

In the Thetford plantations willow tits fed their young chiefly on caterpillars from the pines, and in Marley Wood in 1948 one pair was seen to take caterpillars to the young 231 times and other foods only twice during the whole nestling period. There is little published information about the food of nestling marsh tits in England, but at one nest I watched the adults bring several spiders and unidentified dark objects during the first few days after hatching, but after the first week they appeared to feed the nestlings almost entirely on small green caterpillars. Crested tit nestlings on the other hand seem to eat spiders, earwigs, aphids, hover-flies and moths as well as caterpillars. When feeding young the adults search low bushes and long grass in forest clearings as well as the branches and needle clusters of the pines.

So in spite of a general similarity of the food of all nestling tits there are differences between the *Parus* species in the kinds of invertebrate prey they prefer and in the size of the items they select. The favourite forms of prey vary from one year to another, and at different stages in the same season, and these changes are not always related to the abundance of the prey or to its conspicuousness. L. Tinbergen proposed the concept of 'specific search images' to explain these facts. He suggested that birds tend to overlook kinds of food that are scarce and unfamiliar to them, but when they encounter a certain type of prey more frequently, as it becomes abundant, they form a 'mental image' of this type as the object of their search. Thus the predator tends to specialise temporarily in one kind of food and to ignore others.

Royama formulated the principle of 'profitability' as the basis of the great tit's selection of food for its nestlings. He suggests that the bird tries to get the maximum quantity of food for a given output of hunting effort. The abundance and size of the prey and the hunting methods of the predator would all be taken into account. It remains doubtful whether either of these two theories fully accounts for the varied choice of foods by individual great tits.

The energy and diligence shown by tits in feeding their young has often aroused the admiration of birdwatchers. Casual watching, however, may give a misleading impression of the actual rate of feeding. A pair of blue tits may maintain a rate of one visit a minute for half an hour or more, but they may also stop feeding the nestlings at all for periods of 10–15 minutes. N. D. Pullen's pioneer study of a pair of blue tits with 11 nestlings by the electrical recording of visits probably gives a fair sample of the feeding activity of the smaller *Parus* tits (Table 8).[6] His hourly totals do not show a regular peak of feeding activity at any particular time of day, but at other nests an evening increase has been observed.

TABLE 8   FEEDING FREQUENCY OF BLUE TIT NESTLINGS

Date	First feed	Last feed	Total for day	Average per hour
13/5 (3rd day)	0406 hrs	1945 hrs	396	25
18/5 (8th day)	0400 hrs	1930 hrs	454	30
25/5 (15th day)	0402 hrs	1949 hrs	649	42
27/5 (17th day)	0440 hrs	1926 hrs	601	41*

* This includes a period of reduced activity during four hours of heavy rain.

The extraordinary effort of which a blue tit is capable in an emergency was shown by the male of a pair watched by G. A. and M. A. Arnold.[7] The female disappeared on the 11th day after hatching, but on the 14th day the cock averaged 37 visits per hour, with an estimated daily total of 550–600 visits. Although he was apparently unable to maintain this output of energy and the feeding rate dropped sharply in the last two or three days, he succeeded in fledging 9 out of 10 nestlings.

J. A. Gibb, who studied 52 great tits' nests over a period of four years in Wytham Woods, reported 'enormous variation' in the frequency with which great tits fed their young, even under apparently identical environmental conditions.[8] Changes in temperature did not affect the rate of feeding, but heavy rain slowed it down and might even prevent it altogether for short periods. The parents of large first broods visited the nest more often than parents of small ones, but the frequency of visits to large broods did not increase in proportion to the number of young. Towards the end of the nestling period the young of large or late broods usually received more visits per hour in the morning than in the afternoon and Dr Gibb concluded that the parents were straining in their efforts to maintain the food supply.

However, the frequency of parental visits does not necessarily show the amount of food actually received by the nestlings. Great tits usually, but not always, carry one item at a time, but the size of the prey varies widely and females sometimes visit the nest without food in the first days after the hatching of the eggs, or at any time in late broods. Blue tits sometimes, and marsh and willow tits quite commonly, bring two or three caterpillars at once and coal tits may mix different kinds of prey in one beakful. By the use of an electronically operated camera, T. Royama discovered an inverse relationship between the frequency of visits and the average size of food brought to great tits' nests, so that the weight of food taken to each family was remarkably similar. Nevertheless, weighing of nestlings has confirmed Dr Gibb's impression that chicks in a large brood each receive less food than those in a small one. Except in years when food is unusually abundant, the mean weight of nestling great tits and blue tits is lower in large broods than in small ones, and lower still in great tit second broods in broad-leaved woodland—but not in pines, where food is more plentiful later in the summer.

NESTLING MORTALITY

The belief that tits rear as many young as they can feed is confirmed by the wide differences in the weight and mortality of nestlings in different habitats. Excluding losses from predation, the deaths of great tit nestlings only amounted to 5 per cent of the total hatched in first broods in broad-leaved woods in southern England, but in Scots pine the average was 38 per cent and in gardens 44 per cent. The corresponding figures for blue tits were 4 per cent in oakwoods, 29 per cent in Scots pine and 31 per cent in gardens. Conditions in north-west England seem to be less favourable. Great tits' first brood losses averaged 11 per cent in broad-leaved woods in Cumbria and north Lancashire in 1968–72, and blue tits' 8 per cent. In limestone woods with a mixture of yew and broad-leaved trees great tits' nestling mortality was almost doubled, at 21 per cent.

Nest Record Cards show that, excluding failures of whole broods, willow tits lost 5 per cent of the nestlings they hatched in various habitats (24 broods), marsh tits 10 per cent (52 broods) and Scottish crested tits 15 per cent (7 broods). (The losses of crested tits are surprisingly high considering the small size of the clutches, but a figure based on only 7 nests may be misleading.)

A study of coal tits in Breckland pine plantations showed that their late broods, unlike those of great tits in oakwoods, were better fed than early ones. On average each young coal tit in a first brood received 69 prey items per day, and a second-brood chick received about 50, but items brought to late broods tended to be larger, so that they received nearly twice as much food per day as earlier ones. Fledging success was very high. Excluding a few losses from predation, 98 per cent of the hatched young flew from first broods in Scots pines, and 92 per cent in Corsican pines. For second broods the figures were 99 per cent and 100 per cent respectively. Coal tits breeding in broad-leaved woods also averaged 99 per cent fledging success from first broods. Coal tits in fact seem to be highly efficient parents, and it is surprising that they normally lay smaller clutches of eggs than blue tits.

The nestlings' food requirements are modest compared with those of adults. The deep well-insulated nest, the contact with the rest of the brood and the brooding of the mother during the first few days reduce the heat loss of the chicks to a minimum, and their output of energy is at first very limited. Nestlings in small broods lose more heat than do those of normal families, because each chick has a greater area of body surface exposed to the air. Consequently they need more food to maintain their body heat. Royama found that each chick in a brood of 3 received about 1,750mg of food per day, while one in a brood of 13 received only about 700mg per day. Yet a nestling from a brood of 8 was as heavy as one from a brood of 3, although given much less food. Thus the total time required for parental care of a brood of 3 would only be about 20 per cent less than that needed for a brood of 8. Royama suggested that the main advantage of small broods might come when the young leave the nest, as the activity and heat loss of the fledglings must then be roughly similar to the adults', and they may need a threefold increase in food at this time.

The effect of brood size on the heat loss of nestling great tits has also been studied by Dr J. A. L. Mertens.[9] He found that a single ten-day-old great tit could not maintain its body temperature in a nest at 12° C, but two or more together could do so. At 18° C, 6 or 7 ten-day-old nestlings raised the air temperature to a level at which they were beginning to suffer excessive water loss, and 12 chicks at 12° C produced a similar result. So apart from the difficulty the parents may have in finding sufficient food for abnormally large broods, the effects upon the chicks of hyperthermia in hot weather could be serious. The inside of the lid and sides of nest-boxes containing large broods of well-grown tit nestlings are in fact often dripping with moisture in warm weather. This might be one factor favouring the smaller clutches usual in late nests.

Although eggs and nestlings in holes are much less vulnerable to predation than those in open nests, tits sometimes suffer appreciable casualties. In woodland the most dangerous predator is the weasel, an expert climber and small enough to enter a nest-box through the hole. The stoat similarly attacks nests in larger holes. Locally grey squirrels may enlarge entrance holes by gnawing away the wood, and extract the young; but the most notorious box-wrecker and baby-snatcher is the great spotted woodpecker (plate, page 52). This bird has been known to take the nestlings of several species and is probably responsible for most of the heavy losses of willow tit eggs and nestlings in natural sites: 21 per cent of 58 fully recorded nests in the Nest Record Scheme were opened up. It is only since 1940 that attacks on nest-boxes have been recorded, but damage is now frequent, though irregular, in most parts of Britain. In the first place woodpeckers are probably attracted by the hunger calls of nestlings, but they soon learn to associate the box itself with food and often excavate large holes in the front or sides even in winter and early spring (plate, page 52).

Sometimes a whole brood of young is found dead in the nest. When they have all died at the same age it is unlikely that starvation is the immediate cause, but they may have died from cold during the mother's absence in the search for food. In wet weather casualties of this kind in nest-boxes are not uncommon and they may be due to chilling of the nestlings from dampness of the nest. The death of the mother before the young are feathered may also be fatal for them, and near gardens and orchards there is the possibility of poisoning from chemical insecticides.

On several occasions three, or even four, long-tailed tits have been seen feeding young in the same nest, and it is generally believed that the extra helpers are bereaved parents. In May 1972 Mr C. Scott watched a surprising variation of this behaviour. A long-tailed tit was regularly feeding a brood of young great tits in a hole in an apple tree. When it entered the hole its head and body would disappear, leaving only the tail visible. This transference of parental care is unusual in the *Parus* tits, but one male blue tit with no surviving nestlings was watched feeding a family of young blackbirds for several days,[10] and another regularly fed a brood of young treecreepers, although his mate was feeding their own nestlings on the opposite side of the same tree.[11]

SECOND BROODS

The usual reaction of tits to the loss of a clutch of eggs is to build a new, if sketchy, nest not far away and lay a fresh but smaller clutch. They may also nest again if they lose a brood of small nestlings; indeed, most late nests in Britain are replacements of lost eggs or young. Some pairs of great tits rear genuine second broods, but a much bigger proportion of them do so on the European continent than in Britain. In Holland about 36 per cent of the pairs raised second broods in a broad-leaved wood and about 76 per cent in Scots pines, compared with 2 per cent and 28 per cent in corresponding woods in the south and east of England. Second broods are even less common in the other tits. In Breckland pine plantations up to 5 per cent of the blue tits bred twice,[12] but marsh, willow and crested tits rarely attempt a second brood. However, in 1966 a pair of marsh tits raised two broods in the same nest-box in Hampshire, and at least one second brood of Scottish crested tits has been recorded. In mid-June one sometimes finds a little fresh nesting material placed in previously empty boxes, and these little collections of moss and dead grass may be abortive attempts at second nests by great or blue tits.

H. N. Kluijver found that second broods in Holland were more frequent when population density was low and in years when breeding was early, and older females raised second broods more often than did one-year-olds.[13] He also showed that nearly all pairs of great tits could be induced to rear second broods if the number of fledglings in the first brood was experimentally reduced. The large proportion of second broods in conifers may be linked with the facts that the caterpillar supply continues to increase in the pines until mid-July whereas in oaks it drops sharply after early June, that the density of great tit population is much lower in conifers than in broad-leaved woods, and that first broods in pines generally have poor fledging success. The nestlings of late or second broods in broad-leaved woods are well below average in weight and suffer heavy losses, but those in pines are much more successful. Second-brood eggs are laid, usually in a different nest-hole, almost immediately after the first-brood young have left the nest. In second or late broods the female begins to incubate when only part of the clutch has been laid, so that the young hatch over a period of three or four days. Consequently in case of food shortage the youngest nestlings soon die and the bigger ones have a better chance of survival.

In the Breckland conifer plantations only 9 per cent of the coal tits began second broods in Scots pine and 4 per cent in Corsican pine. These low percentages, in spite of the favourable conditions for second broods and the fact that coal tits nest early, may be due to the good fledging success of the first broods and consequent high population density.

FLEDGING

Although young tits sometimes leave the nest prematurely, for no apparent reason, when they can only flutter downwards from the hole, nestlings have usually been stretching and flapping their wings inside the nest-box or hole for two or three days before they leave, and they are then capable of at least 10 metres level flight. The departure may begin at any time of day, commonly in the morning. Very often the whole brood has left the nest, singly or two or three birds in quick succession, in less than an hour, but occasionally one or two laggards may stay in the hole overnight. There are often signs that a chick requires an effort of will to launch out from the nest-hole. The calls of the parents act as a stimulus. At one great tit's nest in an observation box, two out of five nestlings remained at noon on 7 June, one dozing in the bottom of the nest and the other perched on the side. When an adult called outside, *i-chu, i-chu, i-chu*, both chicks became agitated; one scrambled up to the hole, hesitated a few seconds and then flew. The remaining nestling struggled up against the front corners of the box and then fell back into the nest. Two minutes later an adult put its head through the hole, flew off and began calling. The chick at once fluttered up to the hole and out.

Once they have left the nest the fledglings are more often heard than seen. The hunger calls of young great, blue, coal and marsh tits are generally similar, a rapidly repeated *zicker-zicker* or *tsee-tsee-tsee*, but fledgling willow tits have a harsh begging call written by Foster and Godfrey as *zee-da-da*. The fledglings often accompany their begging-calls with wing shivering of varying intensity, but all immediately relapse into silence on hearing the parents' alarm notes. From the second day they follow the adults from tree to tree and they begin pecking at leaves and twigs after three or four days, though they are almost entirely dependent on their parents for food for a week after leaving the nest. It is normally over a fortnight and sometimes over three weeks before young *Parus* tits are fully independent, and this is a period of great danger and heavy mortality for them.

6 Flocks, Local Movements and Migration

―――――◆―――――

THE WINTER FLOCKS

For two to four weeks after leaving the nest, young tits of all species move about in family parties. Even during the first week after fledging two families of the same species may join up together for a time, but it is after the young have become fully independent that they form the first considerable flocks of mixed species, during the period when the adults are accomplishing their moult. These associations of young birds in July and August are rather loose ones, very variable in size, composition and movements, usually with much chasing and skirmishing. Autumnal display and fighting among great tits have been attributed to the need for young birds to establish territories or 'domiciles' before the winter,[1] but it is noticeable that the young willow warblers which often join these late-summer parties are even more quarrelsome both towards the tits and their own species, and in their case there is no question of territorial claims. These encounters within the mixed flock, which give the impression of juvenile exuberance rather than serious conflict, may establish some sort of order of dominance among the individuals concerned.

By the end of September the tit flocks have become more stable and their ranges more clearly defined. The composition of a flock varies both with the habitat and with the population levels of the different species in a particular year. In some habitats large flocks of a single species may be found. For example a flock of 200–300 great tits was recorded in Lanarkshire in September 1948, and unmixed flocks of about 100 blue tits sometimes occur in reed-beds. Unmixed, but usually smaller, flocks of coal tits are found in conifers. But much more often a flock consists of three or four kinds of tits together with a few fellow-travellers of other species.

One or two marsh tits are commonly found in the winter flocks. There are records of much larger numbers: up to twenty have been recorded in the west Midlands, but these must be regarded as exceptional.[2] Averil Morley showed that the marsh tits in Bagley Wood near Oxford fell into two categories, territory owners and landless birds. A territory-owning pair would not only tolerate a mixed tit flock on its territory but would accompany it as far as the boundary. The landless birds in the flock provided a reservoir from which bereaved territory owners could acquire new mates.

In Britain the willow tit appears to be even less gregarious than the marsh tit. One or two do sometimes occur in winter flocks, but some birds seem to maintain territories through the winter while others wander independently of the mixed flocks. Crested tits are also described as being strictly sedentary and not normally gregarious, but in late August and September I have seen from two to five among mixed tit flocks in several parts of Speyside, and some individuals or pairs associate with coal tits during the winter.

A party of long-tailed tits is an attractive component of many flocks when they are moving through twigs and branches, but they do not join other tits feeding on the ground. The long-tails commonly number 6–20 birds, but over 60 have been reported in a single flock. They generally move from tree to tree more quickly than the *Parus* tits and this may result in their becoming separated from the other species.

Goldcrests often accompany the tits in deciduous woods as well as conifers. A single treecreeper is a very frequent companion even of the smallest tit parties; occasionally there are two but rarely more. Nuthatches and lesser spotted woodpeckers are also represented by single birds if at all. This attraction of the tit flock for single individuals of species not themselves gregarious is a curious phenomenon for which there is no obvious explanation. A ground-feeding flock, especially under beeches in autumn, often mixes with finches, especially chaffinches and bramblings. In late summer and early autumn several species of warblers and sometimes spotted flycatchers and pied fly-catchers may be temporarily present in the tit flocks.

The chief characteristics of an integrated flock are its cohesion, both in feeding and moving, the synchronisation of its activities, and the maintenance of an 'individual distance' between feeding birds which reduces competition for particular items of food. Integration is of course a matter of degree, and gregarious behaviour in the tits has not developed the same perfection as, for example, in some wading birds and geese, but nevertheless, the success with which numbers of small birds of several different species moving through trees keep together over considerable periods is remarkable. Undoubtedly the chief factor in maintaining this cohesion is an auditory one, the constant use of contact notes or flight calls that are generally similar in the different tit species and are uttered with increased frequency when a flock makes a definite move or is just about to do so. R. A. Hinde distinguished two types of flock movement: 'drifting', in which the members of the flock are searching for food as they travel, and 'integrated movements', in which the whole flock may fly 100 metres or more before resuming the hunt for food. A modified form of drifting occurs even in a ground-feeding flock, as the main concentration of tits moves slowly from the foot of one tree to another. Even when there is an abundant local food supply, for example under beech trees in a good mast autumn, the tit flock does not stay very long in the same place, though it may return to a favoured site several times in a day. Integrated movements are not noticeable in coniferous woods.

The route taken by a flock drifting through trees is erratic and un-predictable: the birds may travel in a certain direction for some distance and then turn back and cross their earlier course. R. A. Hinde recorded a maximum speed of under 46m (50 yards) per hour in the summer and autumn of 1949, but in winter the rate was often 183m (200 yards) per hour. J. A. Gibb noted 'drifting' at over 900m (1,000 yards) per hour in pine plantations. Flocks including long-tailed tits tend to move faster than those without. A. J. Gaston found that in winter unmixed parties of long-tails averaged almost 900m (1,000 yards) per hour in mixed woodland, that these flocks were composed of the same individuals through the winter and that they actively defended their territory against other flocks.[3] However, the size and composition of a *Parus* flock may change from day to day or even from hour to hour. Very large flocks, sometimes over 100 birds, do not last long in woodland: they tend to break up into groups of a dozen or less. Winter flocks are normally bigger in the morning than the afternoon and are more closely integrated in cold weather; in mild conditions they may be widely scattered over a considerable area. A flock of *Parus* tits has no definite territorial boundaries and its members show no hostility towards other flocks. Nevertheless a flock with at least a nucleus of the same individuals may be found throughout the winter in a certain area. R. A. Hinde recorded that the range covered by a flock in its travels was normally about 4–8 hectares (10–20 acres). Towards evening the party breaks up as its members disperse to their several roosting holes, situated anywhere within this area.

The dissolution of the flock in spring is a slow and gradual process, usually beginning in January, as various forms of reproductive behaviour—pair formation, song, territorial fighting, visiting nest-holes —become more frequent and the birds spend more time in their preferred area or breeding territory. In mild weather there are sometimes chases between pairs, or prospective pairs, within the flock, but the whole process may be halted by an onset of severe weather in February or March. Usually the flocks have broken up by the end of March but dispersal may be delayed in a cold spring: in the chilly second week of April 1973 all the English *Parus* tits were represented in a well-integrated flock of some 20 birds in a Westmorland birch wood. Even when the territorial rivalry of the breeding season inhibits the assembly of tits of the same species, there are signs that a gregarious tendency still persists; small parties of pairs or individuals of different species not infrequently move around together even in late April and May. These birds are presumably unmated, or are late or frustrated breeders or expectant fathers whose mates are incubating.

It seems clear that tits derive some satisfaction or sense of security from the company of others of their own or similar species, but the survival value of this behaviour is not so clear. It is generally believed that flocking benefits gregarious birds, either by helping them to discover and exploit a food supply, or by providing protection from predators. It has been shown by experiments with great tits in aviaries that a bird searching for food placed in 'clumps' was more likely to be successful when in a flock of four than when alone or in a pair.[4] Once one member of the flock has found food the others tend to assemble round the source and increase their rate of search. They also tend to focus attention on places of the same type as that of the food source. This imitation, or social learning, could be useful to tits in natural conditions where foods like seeds and the eggs of some insects are localised in quantity, but it could hardly help members of a mixed flock drifting through a wood with each species tending to concentrate upon a different part of the tree.

The vocal and visual conspicuousness of a flock of tits would seem to make them more susceptible to predation by hawks than single birds or pairs. However, it is possible that tits in a flock receive earlier warning of impending attack than they would as separate individuals and so can concentrate on looking for food with less need to watch for danger. An incident one November day impressed me with the efficiency of this warning system. A flock of tits was feeding under beech trees at the end of an avenue with no effective and accessible cover except a single dense hawthorn bush about 20 metres away. Suddenly there was a trilling alarm call, followed by others, and within a few seconds 30 blue tits, 6 great tits, 3 coal tits and 1 marsh tit had taken refuge in the hawthorn bush. They remained there, silent, for about two minutes before drifting away in twos and threes. In this case the tits would have been in much greater danger from the passing sparrowhawk if they had been scattered in ones and twos along the beech avenue.

In a study of the interactions between tit flocks and sparrowhawks in woods near Oxford, D. H. Morse found that a sparrowhawk typically attacks when it is below the canopy of the trees before the flock responds to it.[5] Whether the attack is successful or not the hawk makes no second attempt, and the tits usually resume normal activity in less than two minutes. At other times sparrowhawks fly very slowly over the canopy and may repeat this searching flight more than once: on these occasions the tits remain in hiding twice as long. The tit flocks thus seem to have evolved a refuge behaviour adapted to the hunting strategy of the predator. However, this function of flocking provides no explanation of the correlation between cold weather and integrated flock behaviour. Sparrowhawks are presumably as dangerous on mild days when the tits are widely scattered as on cold ones when they are in much closer contact.

LOCAL MOVEMENTS AND MIGRATION

When fledgling tits fly from the nest they usually leave its immediate vicinity and remain quietly concealed for about twenty-four hours. During the following ten to fifteen days the family does not move far from the former parental territory, although this is no longer defended. In the Netherlands, Kluijver found that only one out of 57 families of great tits moved more than 800 metres from the nest, and the maximum range for the majority was 200–400 metres. It is when the juveniles become fully independent that some significant movement of great and blue tits begins.

The dispersal of young birds seems to be gradual and continuous in late summer and autumn. In 1950 I. M. Goodbody marked with coloured rings the nestling blue and great tits in nest-boxes in Marley Wood and plotted their subsequent distribution up to mid-September.[6] About the end of June 72 per cent of the young great tits in Marley Wood were ringed but only 8 per cent in an adjoining strip of woodland called The Singing Way; by the end of August 22 per cent of those in The Singing Way were ringed but only 37 per cent of those in Marley Wood. Blue tits showed a similar gradual dispersal. A few ringed tits were seen up to a mile (1·6km) away in July and August. In mid-August there were signs of a considerable influx of unringed tits. Similar movements of numbers of blue and great tits about this time are noticeable in other parts of Britain, but the ringing recoveries summarised below suggest that in a normal year most of these birds have probably not travelled far.

In a study of great tits in Wytham Woods, Dr C. M. Perrins recorded that out of 5,784 nestlings ringed, some 614 had been recovered inside the Wytham estate and only 45 outside.[7] The majority of the latter group was found near houses within 5km (3 or 4 miles) of Wytham, and some of these may still have been roosting in the wood.

Very few fully adult great tits were recovered away from the wood. A tit that has once nested in a certain area rarely moves far from it.

The recoveries of tits ringed in the British Isles show that only a very small proportion of them travel long distances. An analysis of the recoveries of great and blue tits from 1959 until the end of 1968 showed that only 3 per cent of great tits, and 2·2 per cent of blue tits had moved more than 30 miles (48km) in the British Isles. British-ringed great tits were only recovered abroad in 4 of the 10 years and blue tits in only 1 year. A small number of journeys of over 30 miles by birds identified as 'adult' have been recorded: the great majority were made by tits known to be less than a year old or simply recorded as 'full-grown'.[8]

The limited extent of most tit movements is confirmed on a local scale by L. A. Cowcill at his ringing station at the foot of Coniston Water, Cumbria. Of 386 great tits ringed over ten years, only 1 was recovered more than 5km away. Of 545 blue tits ringed, 4 were recovered over 5km from the trapping station, 3 of them at Barrow-in-Furness 21km SSW (2 of these in mid-winter), while 2 ringed at Barrow in mid-March were 'controlled' (the ringer's term for a bird caught and released) a few days later by Coniston Water and subsequently retrapped there. These could well be examples of a regular movement of blue tits into towns from rural areas for winter feeding and back for breeding, though the distance involved is surprising. C. M. Perrins mentions 2 blue tits known to have travelled 18 and 32km from Wytham Wood and to have returned there the following summer.

Cowcill found that several blue and great tits released in the same valley up to 8km from the trapping station returned to it in one to five days, but those released further away never reappeared. In Germany, Creutz tried homing experiments with many great and blue tits and found that 40 per cent of tits released within 4km of the place of capture returned, but only 10 per cent of those released between 4 and 6·5km away. So most tits only know the topography of a very limited area around their home range.

Few ringing recoveries give definite indications of the directions of spring and autumn movements of more than 48km (30 miles) in the British Isles, but of 8 blue tits ringed in presumed winter quarters

7 had moved to points between NE and SE in spring, and of 13 ringed in their presumed breeding area 8 had travelled to the north or west or points between in autumn. These directions are in accord with the trends shown by tits in 'irruption' years. On the continent the general direction of travel in autumn is between west and south, so this marked northerly tendency in the British Isles is difficult to explain. However, in effect the NW bearing helps to spread immigrants and southern-bred tits over the whole of Great Britain, whereas an SW one would have funnelled them into a restricted and comparatively treeless area. If continued far enough, NW movements would also offer some climatic advantages, in view of the milder, comparatively snow-free winters in the north-west and the warmer, drier summers in the east.

Great tits recovered within the British Isles show a less consistent pattern than blue tits, but there are again indications of a trend towards the north and west in autumn and the east in spring. An interesting record is that of a great tit ringed as a first-winter bird in Cambridge on 5 November 1966, 'controlled' 56km SSE in Essex on 17 March 1967 and recovered back in Cambridge about 1 February 1968—perhaps an Essex-born bird which discovered good town feeding in its first-winter northerly travels, returned 'home' to breed and went back to Cambridge for its second winter. Such an ability to re-discover a feeding-place 56km away would be noteworthy.

Comparatively small numbers of tits of other species are ringed and recovered in the British Isles. Out of 107 coal tits recovered between 1959 and 1968, 2 had made inland movements of between 48 and 129km, and a third, ringed on the Essex coast in April 1960, was found on a light-ship 80km to the east in May of the same year.

No movements of more than 5km have been recorded for marsh tits ringed in Britain, although 8,411 had been ringed and 68 recovered up to and including 1969, nor for willow tits (6,641 ringed and 37 recovered). Up to 1972 there had been no recoveries of Scottish crested tits from the 134 ringed. The fact that these three species are strongly sedentary is underlined by their distribution in the British Isles and their slowness to colonise apparently suitable habitats not far from established populations. This reluctance to travel may be at least partly responsible for the slow spread of the Scottish crested tit, and perhaps also for the very patchy distribution of the willow tit, which is completely absent from birch and alder woods in some parts of the country while well distributed in apparently similar ones in a neighbouring county. The marsh tit is abundant in the woods of south Westmorland but is not found in others of the same type in north Westmorland and Cumberland, although it occurs much further north on the east of the Pennines. In this case the few kilometres of open mountainous country in the Lake District seem to act as an effective barrier to expansion. It is also significant that neither marsh nor willow tits have been recorded in the Isles of Scilly, or, with one possible exception, in the Isle of Man. This sedentary behaviour seems to have psychological rather than physical causes. Both marsh and willow tits appear to have a stronger and less laboured flight than blue tits; they not infrequently fly swiftly and directly from end to end of their comparatively extensive territories, while blue tits tend to move in much shorter stages from tree to tree. In some parts of northern Europe willow tits may make much longer journeys, and a few individual marsh and crested tits are occasionally caught up in big 'irruption' movements. A continental crested tit, for example, reached the Scillies in 1970.

It may seem surprising that the long-tailed tit, with its tiny body, short wings and heavy ballast of tail feathers should be a comparatively frequent traveller over moderate distances, but recent ringing recoveries show this to be the case. In the ten years 1959–68, 7 of the 124 recoveries of long-tailed tits, 5·7 per cent, were more than 48km from the place of ringing. This is higher than the average for any of the *Parus* tits. In some years long-tailed tits reach the south and east coasts of England from the continent. In October 1961, 7 out of a flock of 8 were ringed together in Lincolnshire and were netted together 43km away four days later, a nice example of flock or family cohesion.

In certain years there are large-scale movements of tits of several species in northern and central Europe, involving many thousands of birds in journeys of at least three or four hundred kilometres. One of these 'invasions' or 'irruptions' which affected the British Isles to an exceptional extent was in autumn 1957, and another, more marked in Scandinavia and central Europe, in autumn 1959. Both movements have been carefully documented, by Cramp, Pettet and Sharrock in 1960 and by Cramp in 1963.[9]

In 1957 there were reports of large numbers and unusual movements of blue and great tits in various parts of England, chiefly in the south, between late June and mid-August, before there was any indication of immigration from overseas. The arrival of continental migrants on the east and south coasts began about the middle of September, reached a peak in early October and had almost ceased by mid-November. Blue tits were much the most numerous immigrants and in some places they were seen in large numbers, for example 447 travelling NW at Sandwich Bay, Kent, on 27 September, over 460 at Portland on the 28th, and 600 moving south at Hunstanton, Norfolk, in 1½ hours on 13 October. The numbers of great tits seen in 1957 were generally smaller, but some considerable counts in the south included 150 at Portland and about 200 in the Channel Islands, both on 7 October. Coal tits on the other hand were generally more numerous in the north than the south. Parties of tits travelled as far north-west as the Inner Hebrides and there was evidence that some reached Ireland. A return movement of blue and great tits towards the SE was noticeable from January to mid-May 1958.

Coastal influxes of long-tailed tits in October were reported, and increases were observed in Ireland and the Channel Islands. Up to 3 marsh tits were seen together on the coast in four places in the south of England, but there is no proof that these were of continental origin.

Recoveries of British-ringed blue and great tits confirmed the exceptional nature of the movements in 1957–8; 29 (6·2 per cent) out of 470 blue tits recovered had travelled over 48km (30 miles), and 9 (5·7 per cent) of 157 great tits. These percentages compare with averages of 1·6 and 2·1 respectively for all recoveries up to 1956. All 5 of the presumed British native blue tits which had been ringed in southern and central England and had travelled over 30 miles had moved between NW and NNE. One ringed in Flanders was recovered in Yorkshire. Blue, great and coal tits ringed in autumn and winter and recovered in the following spring and summer showed a trend in the reverse direction and include several found in N France, the Low Countries and NW Germany.

On the continent, large-scale movements of blue, great and coal tits, with some long-tailed and a few crested and marsh tits were reported from coastal and inland districts of NW Germany, the Netherlands and Belgium between mid-August and November 1957. The general trend of flight in the autumn was westerly, and an easterly return migration was seen in February and March 1958.

The irruption of 1959 was on a much smaller scale in Britain, but arrivals of blue tits on the east and south coasts of England and of great tits in Scotland were above average. In Sweden, Norway and Heligoland the movements of blue and great tits were much bigger than in 1957, there was a very heavy passage in Switzerland and large numbers in southern France. A coal tit ringed in Saxony was recovered over 1,600km away on the east coast of Spain: this is the longest known journey for the species.

Although irruptions of tits into the British Isles on the scale of 1957 are exceptional there is some evidence of other invasions both before 1957 and after 1959. It is known that great tits are regular autumn immigrants to Britain in moderate numbers, while continental blue tits are comparatively scarce and coal tits are only occasional visitors. S. Cramp showed that immigrants to Britain usually come from the low-lying areas of north-west Europe, crossing the North Sea or the English Channel.

There has been much discussion of the causes of the occasional eruptive movements by large numbers of birds like the waxwing, crossbill and some of the tits. David Lack suggested that food shortage was the 'ultimate factor' in all eruptive movements, but he pointed out that while the minor emigrations were a direct response to a poor fruit crop the big ones might be stimulated by a behaviour response to high numbers and might start before food became scarce.[10] The major tit emigrations, like that of 1957, have occurred in years when the breeding population of tits has been high.

G. Svärdson, dealing chiefly with waxwings, crossbills, siskins and fieldfares, takes a different view of eruptive movements.[11] He regards them as basically a form of normal migration which is inhibited in years when food is abundant. He suggests that eruptive species start a flight every year, stimulated by the same factors as ordinary migrants, but stop when they find a good food supply. He has shown that

A long-tailed tit at the nest

Page 102 (*left*) A marsh tit, identifiable by its pale flanks and thick bill; and (*right*) seen at the nest-hole

certain seed crops, valuable to birds, tend to vary in parallel from year to year. Spruce, beech and birch in particular tend to have an alternating rhythm of good and bad crops, and all three of these had a very poor yield in Sweden in 1949, when there was a large autumnal movement of tits.

C. M. Perrins has pointed out that one result of the tendency to alternate-year fruiting is that, as more birds survive the winter after a good autumn crop, the population of breeding tits is likely to be high the following summer, when the developing beech-mast crop will inevitably be small.[12] This makes it difficult to determine whether an eruption in one of these years is due to high population or to shortage of food. Thus the number of breeding pairs of great and blue tits both in England and the Netherlands was unusually high in 1957. But Perrins shows that the actual number of great tits surviving until the autumn in Marley Wood, Oxford, was below average in the irruption years.

Long-term records show that continental great tit populations, at least in the Netherlands, tend to fluctuate in parallel with the Oxford ones, so it seems likely that eruptions do not occur in years of high population density but in years when the seed crops have failed. It may be added that big movements of coal tits have coincided with those of crossbills and a failure of the seed crop of the Norway spruce.

Dr Perrins makes two other interesting suggestions. One is that from an evolutionary point of view alternate-year cropping is to the advantage of the tree species, as the 'seed-predators' are reduced in number by starvation in one year and provided with a surfeit the following one, so that many seeds are left to germinate. The other is that irruptions of tits into Britain and western Europe may become more common as the growing number of garden feeding-stations enables more of the immigrants to survive. The advantage to the species of autumn migration to areas of dense human population may thus be steadily increasing.

The relationship between beech crops and the survival of tits will be discussed further in Chapter 13.

7 Feeding and Food-storing

FEEDING

When the fledgling tits leave the nest both they and their parents acquire a new freedom. The adults can lead their family to an abundant food supply instead of having to carry each item, often singly, over distances of as much as two or three hundred metres. In the first few days the whole brood is often collected into a single tree and the parents feed their fledglings with impressive speed and efficiency and with much less expenditure of energy than was required during the nestling period. Smaller food items such as aphids become 'economic', and by the time the juveniles are fully independent they are probably acquainted with a fair variety of foods.

Soon after the family parties break up some young blue and great tits begin to move away from the breeding area, as was shown in the previous chapter. These journeys are usually short, but may take the birds into completely different habitats. Blue tits seem to be attracted by low-lying land with willows and reed-beds, and both blue and great tits may be found in autumn and winter searching hedgerows in open country they would not visit in the breeding season. Occasionally one or two willow tits appear in the hedges, either in a mixed flock or by themselves. Many blue tits also move into plantations of Scots pine and other conifers, although this is an unfavourable breeding habitat for them and they are rarely seen there in spring and early summer. Increasing numbers of blue tits, and some great and coal tits, also move into towns and villages in winter to enjoy easy pickings on bird-tables. On the other hand, long-tailed tits, which tend to breed chiefly in hedgerows, scrubland and woodland fringes and clearings, spend most of the winter actually in the woods, both broad-leaved and coniferous.

The apparent heavy mortality among juvenile great tits in late summer and early autumn has been generally attributed, directly or indirectly, to food shortage (to be discussed in Chapter 13). To the human eye, and skin, insect life seems so superabundant at this season that it is hard to envisage any insectivorous bird starving, but the fact that there are more insects in the flying imago stage might mean that there are less of the larvae and pupae which are often the principal objects of tits' hunting methods. Moreover, the juveniles are inexperienced in finding food and vulnerable to predators while searching for it. In or before September, as the season of 'mellow fruitfulness' approaches, tits turn to seeds and berries, most of which are taken mainly, or entirely, by one species only—for example hazel nuts by great tits, haws by blue tits, honeysuckle seeds, extracted from the berries, by marsh tits and hemp nettle (*Galeopsis*) seeds by willow tits.

This concentration by the different species on particular kinds of vegetable food provides a good illustration of the principle of 'ecological isolation' or 'competitive exclusion'. 'Two species of animals can co-exist in the same area only if they differ in ecology,' to quote David Lack.[1] Careful study has shown that although different species of birds feeding in the same place may appear to be competing for the same food there are usually marked differences in their diet. Dr Lack shows that related species of birds are segregated in three main ways: (a) by geographical range, (b) by habitat, or (c) by food selection. As an example from the tit family, the blue tit, a bird of broad-leaved woodland in western, central and southern Europe, is segregated (a) from the closely related azure tit of Russia by geographical range, (b) from the crested tit, a bird of coniferous forest, by habitat, and (c) from the marsh tit by food.

There is one conspicuous exception to the rule of specialised feeding in the tit family: beech-mast, when plentiful, forms a major part of the diet of great, coal, marsh and blue tits from mid-September to January. At first the nuts are extracted from the husks on the trees, at which operation coal tits seem to be particularly adept, but from mid-October most of the nuts are found on the ground and it is then that the mixed tit flocks under beech trees are in evidence. However, David Lack has pointed out that segregation of species by feeding habits chiefly comes into operation when food is scarce and tends to lapse in periods of temporary abundance. And even under beech trees differences in feeding methods can be detected. In October and November many of the beech nuts are hidden under fallen leaves, but great tits regularly throw these leaves aside with a vigorous jerk of the head and then search the newly exposed ground. (One has been seen to throw aside flat stones in the same way to get at crumbs.) Coal, and more rarely blue and marsh, tits will pick up dead leaves and drop them, but it is an ineffectual performance compared with the great tits'. In effect the great tits are finding beech nuts which are virtually inaccessible to the other species.

When the beech crop fails or has been seriously depleted, and wood-land tits have to search elsewhere for food, even casual watching will reveal certain differences in feeding methods. An example of this is 'vertical zonation', or the tendency of the different species to feed at different heights in the trees. Great tits, for instance, except when feeding young, tend to spend much time on the ground or searching the base of tree trunks or mossy stone walls, while blue and coal tits are the species to be found most often in the upper and outer twigs of tall trees. There are also specific differences in preference for certain kinds of tree and in the part of it—trunk, branch, twig, bud, leaf or flower—most favoured at a particular season. These preferences, and they are preferences rather than hard and fast divisions, have been studied in detail in broad-leaved woods near Oxford by P. H. T. Hartley and J. A. Gibb.[2]

Hartley found that the height distribution of the tit species in the trees varied with the season, and to some extent from year to year. Great tits fed mainly on the ground from December to March, went up into the trees for the caterpillar harvest of early summer, searched the lower foliage in high summer, and in autumn fed high or low according to the abundance of aphids, beech-mast and other foods. Blue tits showed great diversity; in winter especially they were scattered from the lowest shrubs to the tops of the highest trees. In mid-summer the highest levels were deserted, but only when there was an abundant harvest of fallen nuts or fruits did they feed on the ground with any frequency. Coal tits generally fed at a fairly high level in spring and summer, but were dispersed in autumn through a wide range of heights and dropped lower in midwinter. They generally fed higher than blue tits from April to November, lower than blue tits from December to March. The marsh tit had the most clearly defined height distribution of the species studied, feeding at all seasons in the shrub layer and on the lowest limbs of the big trees. Long-tailed tits had a considerable range of feeding levels but rarely fed on the ground and not often in the highest twigs. In general they hunted the top of the shrub layer and the lower strata of the woodland canopy.

Taking the general idea of 'vertical zonation' into further detail, J. A. Gibb recorded the actual part of the tree in which the tits were feeding and the species of tree most favoured by each kind of tit. There were marked seasonal changes in the part of the tree chiefly used. In order of preference hazel, oak, elder and beech were the most important trees for great tits; oak, birch, hazel and elder for blue tits; oak, ash, beech and birch for coal tits, and oak, elder, hazel and beech for marsh tits.

It is also possible that even birds feeding in the same part of the same tree may be taking different foods; for when tits are searching twigs or buds it may be difficult to detect what they are actually eating. Often this question can only be answered by an analysis of stomach or gizzard contents. Monica Betts undertook a study of the food of tit-mice in oak woodland in the Forest of Dean by means of gizzard analyses.[3] These showed that great tits fed mainly on adult insects, especially weevils, while blue tits took mostly scale insects and small larvae and pupae. Coal tits showed a preference for small free insects and scales. Marsh tits took adult insects, scales and some larvae. All four species took a small proportion of spiders and, from July to the end of the winter, galls of various species. Great and marsh tits fed more on seeds than did the other tits, but it was only blue tits that took sporogonia of mosses, which are rich in oil. Blue tits were also specialists in oak-bud tissue. Between February and April, inclusive, 53 out of 54 blue tits had eaten this tissue, and in 34 of these the volume of it was estimated at over 50 per cent of the total gizzard contents. Only 1 great tit and 2 marsh tits had a considerable quantity of bud tissue. Long-tailed tits are mainly insectivorous throughout the year, though some seeds are occasionally taken.

Dr Betts also found differences in the average size of the food items taken by four tit species, and the following table shows the sizes of insect prey graded by length in millimetres.

TABLE 9   SIZE OF INSECT PREY OF *PARUS* SPECIES IN ENGLISH OAK WOOD
PERCENTAGE OF PREY OF EACH SIZE

Size range	Coal tit	Blue tit	Great tit	Marsh tit
0–2mm	74	59	27	22
3–4mm	17	29	20	52
5–6mm	3	3	22	16
Over 6mm	7	10	32	11

The birds' size and weight and the structure of their bills are adapted to the size and type of food that they eat, the great tit taking the largest and hardest items and the coal tit, with its comparatively thin fine bill, the smallest and softest. But it must be emphasised that although these differences reduce the competition between species they do not entirely eliminate it. There is still a considerable overlap in foods taken, as well as in feeding sites and methods, and this overlap is not restricted to periods of abundance. For example, in the first week of April, I watched one great, two blue, two coal and two marsh tits all picking aphids off sycamore buds, although I could only find an average of one aphis to thirty buds on the lower branches. The great tit generally hunted on lower branches than the others but was sometimes above the blue tits, and for some time a marsh tit was in the highest twigs above the coal tits. This kind of peaceful competition for a limited food supply must often occur in winter. Lack has suggested that incomplete segregation of species could be explained by the comparatively recent development of the man-made environment that is found today even in the most rural parts of the British Isles and most of western Europe.

One should also remember that the three studies briefly summarised above refer to selected broad-leaved woods in the south of England (conifer plantations will be considered later), and the feeding habits of tits may not be identical in other types of woods and other parts of the British Isles. For instance, W. B. Yapp describes the conspicuous and destructive attacks of marsh tits on oak buds in late autumn in the Forest of Wyre, Worcestershire,[4] but nothing of the kind is mentioned in the Oxford studies or in the Forest of Dean, and I have not observed it in north-west England. Moreover, oak was the only bud tissue found in tits' gizzards in the Forest of Dean, but elsewhere, although oak is still the commonest object of attack, the buds of several other trees and shrubs are sometimes eaten even when oak is available. In the springs of 1970–2 I observed blue tits in Westmorland attacking oak buds on 40 occasions, elm on 12, pear on 6, and buds of 6 other tree species from 1 to 4 times. Coal tits took blackthorn buds twice and elm once; marsh tits ate oak buds twice and blackthorn once.

In view of this apparent preference for oak buds in natural conditions it was surprising to find little or no evidence of it in a blue tit with an injured wing that I kept loose in a room with an easily accessible large vase of mixed twigs, in addition to peanuts and fat. The first choice offered, on 26 March, consisted of single small branches of roughly similar size of oak, elm, apple, pear, cherry, hawthorn and pussy willow *Salix caprea*. From the first the bird spent much time hopping about in the twigs and by 29 March it had eaten 9 cherry buds, 7 apple, 5 pear, 4 hawthorn, 3 oak, 2 pussy willow. Almost the whole of each bud had been eaten: a few outer scales were sometimes left attached to the twig, but there was no fallen litter round the vase. In a later test, 6 beech and 3 oak buds were eaten out of a selection of oak, elm, beech, birch and larch. Finally, when the tit had recovered its powers of flight and was released, it had eaten 6 terminal oak buds and 5 blackcurrant 'big buds' from a choice of oak, elm, lime, and blackcurrant. Either this bird failed to recognise oak buds away from the tree, or there is some unknown factor in the preference shown by blue tits for oak 'in the field'. Much has still to be learnt about the recognition and selection of food by birds.

In addition to minor regional differences in the feeding habits of tits there may be local variations in vegetation which radically affect their ecology. Around the southern fringe of the English Lake District is an area of carboniferous limestone which often takes the form of wooded hills with a steep escarpment on one side. The broad-leaved woodland on these hills is varied in composition, in some places chiefly ash and hazel coppice, in others standard oak, ash, sycamore and birch with an admixture of other trees and shrubs, but a constant feature of nearly all the woods is the cluster of old yews on the escarpment and other areas of exposed rock and scree. From late summer to spring the yew seeds form a very important part of the diet of great and marsh tits. From August to October these two species, especially the latter, pick the ripe berries from the trees, extract the hard seed, hammer it open on a branch and eat the kernel. During these months berries are taken by several species of the thrush family, but the seeds are voided undigested and may later be used by great and marsh tits. The flocks of thrushes do not clear the whole crop and through the winter, even into April, shrivelled, blackened berries holding viable seeds remain on the female yew trees, while others litter the ground beneath. During this period both great and marsh tits can often be seen picking the seeds from the twigs or off the ground and then hammering them open. The marsh tits also store many seeds. Other types of food are taken by both species, especially birch catkins and small items from oak branches by marsh tits and other unidentified food on or near the ground by great tits, but well over two-thirds of my observations of these two species between October and March have been in or under yew trees.

Both these tits seem to prefer yew seeds to other vegetable food. In some of the limestone woods hazel nuts, an important food of great tits in the south of England, are abundant in most autumns, but they are nearly all left to the red squirrels. Perhaps this is because a great tit takes about 20 minutes to split a hazel nut and only 15–60 seconds to open a yew seed—admittedly for a much smaller reward. I once saw a coal tit swallow an unripe green yew berry in July, but otherwise blue and coal tits have shown no interest in the berries or seeds.

The importance of the yew tree to great and marsh tits is shown by the comparative winter populations of the four common *Parus* species in limestone (yew) and acid (non-yew) woods in the same general area. The kind of broad-leaved trees present in the wood had no detectable influence on the tit populations.

The following table summarising the totals of tits seen in winter on slow walks through woods of the two types in 1970 and 1971 should give a fair impression of the comparative abundance of the species.

TABLE 10

TITS IDENTIFIED IN 14 LIMESTONE WOODS, WITH YEWS, OCTOBER–MARCH

Minutes of transects	Great tit	Blue tit	Coal tit	Marsh tit
1020	126	51	26	89
Mean contacts per hour	7·4	3·0	1·5	5·2

TITS IN 8 WESTMORLAND OAK OR BIRCH WOODS, NO YEWS, SAME PERIOD

Minutes of transects	Great tit	Blue tit	Coal tit	Marsh tit
620	25	45	26	8
Mean contacts per hour	2·4	4·4	2·5	0·8

The yew-seed diet very effectively segregates great and marsh tits, which can hammer open the seeds, from blue and coal which apparently cannot, but some competition between the two former species for the dwindling supply of seeds in early spring seems inevitable.

In a study of the breeding-bird community of the Kingley Vale yew wood in Sussex, R. Williamson and K. Williamson reported that the 'great tit was almost three times commoner than the blue tit, a reversal of the situation found in most kinds of broad-leaved woodland in England; indeed at Kingley Vale the marsh tit was almost as common as the blue tit'.[5] These figures may reflect a link between the populations of great and marsh tits and the supply of yew kernels in winter. It would be interesting to have data from the yew and beech woods of the North Downs.

An exceptionally, and unnaturally, homogeneous woodland habitat is provided by plantations of single species of conifers. J. A. Gibb and his colleagues made a detailed study over a period of more than five years of tits and goldcrests and their food supply in plantations of Scots and Corsican pine in the Thetford Chase Forest on the Norfolk/ Suffolk boundary.[6] Coal tits were much the commonest bird species in the pines in autumn, blue tits were about one-third as numerous, great, willow and long-tailed tits each about one-eighth. In mid-winter the proportion of blue to coal tits was about the same, but long-tailed tits had increased to about a quarter, willow tits had declined to less than one-tenth and great tits were almost absent. At this season there were only about 20 tits per 10 hectares in the pine plantations compared with about 40 per 10 hectares in a mixed broad-leaved wood (Marley). Coal tits were about ten times as numerous in the pines as in broad-leaved woodland and willow tits about twice, but numbers of blue and great tits were much smaller in conifers and marsh tits were absent. All species fed in Scots pines much more than in Corsican.

As in broad-leaved woodland there were seasonal variations in the parts of the trees used for feeding by the different species, but in the critical midwinter period from November to February about two-thirds of the foraging activity of all the birds (including goldcrests) in pine plantations was concentrated in the living foliage. Gibb comments that in both pine and broad-leaved woods each species occupies a recognisable niche, but this niche is much less distinct in pines than in broad-leaved woods. Consequently there must be some inter-specific competition, for instance between blue and coal tits for the larvae of the eucosmid moth *Ernarmonia conicolana* in the scales of pine cones.

In the coniferous forests of Norway S. Haftorn found that crested tits fed at all heights in spruce and pine trees, almost entirely in the branches, especially the outer twigs and needles; they very rarely searched the trunks.[7] In spring and autumn they spent much time on the ground. In Scotland, however, crested tits are often seen searching the trunks of the pines: there seems to be a regional, or racial, difference in feeding habits.

In addition to a variety of vegetable matter, tits take a very wide range of invertebrate animal food, including chironomid midges which are frequently caught in flight, especially in spring and autumn. I have watched all the British tits feeding in this way.

Tits have long enjoyed a reputation for adaptability in their diet and feeding methods, and one macabre variation in particular deserves mention here. A topic of some interest to earlier writers was the alleged murderous tendency of great tits. Howard Saunders wrote that 'the Great Titmouse will attack small and weakly birds, splitting their skulls with its powerful beak in order to get at their brains; and it has even been known to serve a Bat in this manner.'[8] There is no doubt that great tits can kill other birds in this way. I have known two or three cases of pied flycatchers' being found dead with smashed skulls in nest-boxes taken over by great tits; but nearly all the published records are of birds in traps or cages. An interesting exception is an incident in Cumberland described by J. L. Caris.[9] On a bitter day in January a great tit was seen flying heavily with something in its claws. This was found to be a goldcrest, recently killed by a peck at the back of the skull, with both eyes pecked out and the head badly torn.

Heinz Sielmann has filmed a blue tit drinking sap from holes in a tree trunk made by a woodpecker, and C. K. Mylne has recorded blue, coal, marsh and long-tailed tits drinking the sap oozing from a broken twig of silver birch on several successive days in April.[10] They were apparently attracted by the sweetness as well as the moisture. In gardens tits will eat crystallised honey and drink solutions of honey and sugar from phials.

Another occasional and rather surprising food, of which I have not seen any published mention, is the green algal growth (probably *Pleurococcus* or *Chlorella* spp) on the bark of sycamore and some other deciduous trees. This is especially favoured by long-tailed tits, and on many occasions in winter and early spring I have watched small parties of them tapping rapidly and repeatedly on the algae-covered bark of the boles of sycamore or ash saplings or the upper branches of the trees, concentrating on an area of a few square millimetres for several seconds at a time. On one occasion six long-tailed tits were feeding simultaneously like this on the trunk of the same 5-metre sapling, and I have seen seven behaving in the same way on a branch of wych elm. The characteristic intensive tapping is conspicuously different from the selective pecking the birds use when taking aphids or insects' eggs. I have two records of coal tits feeding on young sycamore trunks and branches in exactly the same way in winter, and seven of blue tits, on sycamore, ash and birch. It was noticeable that the blue tits were attacking the scattered green patches on the birch trunks and ignoring the smooth silvery areas. Mr E. G. Williams, to whom I sent, for examination by microscope, samples of sycamore bark worked by long-tailed tits, could find no trace of animal life on them. He drew my attention to the work done on fat accumulation by algae by Professor G. E. Fogg, who tells me that three of the species he studied were likely to occur on tree trunks and 'each of these could accumulate as much as a third of its dry weight in the form of fat. The conditions leading to fat accumulation are shortage of combined nitrogen and desiccation, both of which conditions are very likely to occur on tree trunks . . . It does seem to me likely that birds could derive a considerable amount of nourishment both in the form of protein and fat from algae on tree trunks.'

Just as the diet of all tits shows a general similarity, yet with each species showing special preferences, so their actions in feeding are alike in their vigour and agility but differ in detail. The feeding methods of each species are related to its weight, build and diet. They all hang upside down to pick food from twigs and leaves, but great tits do this chiefly when feeding in the tree tops in late summer or when taking suspended food at a feeding-station, while long-tailed tits seem definitely to prefer this attitude at all seasons. All the *Parus* tits hold seeds and other objects under or between the feet to peck or tear them, insects being generally held under one foot and seeds between the feet. Experiments with hand-reared great tits showed that fledglings tried to hold large items on a perch almost at once but took several weeks' practice to develop the same skill as adults.[11]

The long-tailed tit has an entirely different method of dealing with hard items. Mrs J. Hall-Craggs has described how the bird hangs upside down from a twig and holds the piece of food in one foot 'just as a child might eat an apple'.[12] Softer items are beaten or rubbed against the perch from above. Great and marsh tits are expert in smashing seeds by hammering them with the whole weight of the body 'swinging from the hips': indeed, all the pecking and tearing actions of marsh tits seem to be performed with a characteristic vigour and determination. Coal and crested tits feed chiefly by comparatively gentle picking, pecking and probing, and the methods of willow tits are generally similar. The feeding actions of blue tits are particularly varied and adaptable, but they seem more addicted to the tearing of bark than the other species.

FOOD-STORING

Back in 1797 Thomas Bewick noted that the marsh tit 'lays up a little store of seeds against a season of want'. But this interesting behaviour has been curiously overlooked or ignored in later standard works, and it is surprising not to find any reference to it in Coward or even in

Witherby's authoritative *Handbook*, although similar actions by the corvids are described in both books.[13, 14] Yet any observant feeder of garden birds will notice that coal and marsh tits often fly off some distance with any loose pieces of nut only to return for more in half a minute or less, while great and blue tits eat such fragments on a nearby twig. A few minutes' watching under a mature beech tree in a good mast autumn will often reveal a similar situation. All four common tit species take nuts up to twigs and branches to eat, but some of the coal tits can be seen working their way up through the branches and then flying off, perhaps to some dense evergreen or ivy-covered tree or wall. They usually hold a nut by the apex, and the tiny, short-tailed birds with their projecting load show a curious and characteristic profile in flight. Marsh tits normally carry off their stores at a lower level. Further observation will show that both species are storing away their nuts in a variety of hiding places.

Both blue and great tits have been recorded hiding food, but storing by these two species must be regarded as exceptional. It is probably significant that they, unlike the storing species, sometimes undertake local movements of some kilometres. Food hoarding would only be a profitable activity for a sedentary species. In the Norwegian forests S. Haftorn found that coal, crested and willow tits stored, in the middle area of the trees which would be relatively free of snow in winter, seeds and dead or immobilised invertebrates. Crested tits used saliva to fix seeds in lichen on main branches; coal tits stored food in bud capsules and among needles; willow tits used lichen on trunks and thick branches. Each species was storing food in the part of the tree in which it normally searched during the winter. Consequently it was unnecessary for a bird to remember the location of individual items: the hidden food would serve as a collective winter reserve for all members of the species in a given area. Analysis of the stomach contents of crested and willow tits collected in January and February showed that on average more than half the food of both species must have been stored. Haftorn concluded that stored food was essential for the survival of these three species, and also of the Siberian tit, through the winter.

Conditions of climate and habitat in Britain differ in several respects from those of Haftorn's study area in Norway. I have not seen any published records of food-concealment by Scottish crested tits, but a visit to Speyside in mid-October showed that they are in fact diligent storers of surplus food. When the tits were feeding in the pines food-storing did not appear to be frequent and it could easily be over-looked, but twice within two minutes I saw one bird push small unidentified objects into tufts of lichen growing on the underside of thin dead branches. The second time it worked for about fifteen seconds and may well have been using saliva as an adhesive.

On two successive days I put out a handful of peanut fragments on the ground on the edge of a clearing in the forest where a crofter had been feeding birds, and the results were spectacular. Within a few minutes some thirty or forty coal tits and at least three crested tits were dropping down on the nuts in rapid succession and carrying pieces off into the trees. The coal tits hid them in bark crevices on the trunks of big pines, in splintered dead branches, in lichen on the tops and sides of birch and pine branches, and most of all in a tangle of dead lichened twigs on a nearby pine. Only one bird hid food on the ground, three successive pieces in a hummock of moss and bilberry. Crested tits also chiefly used the tangle of pine twigs, but hid other fragments in the bark of pine trunks, splintered branches and lichen on both pines and birches. Both species stored almost entirely between 2 and 8 metres above the ground and within 40 metres of the food supply. In May I have watched Speyside coal tits hiding pine seeds and unidentified items found among the needles, probably invertebrate food, between 1 and 15 metres up in the bark of trunks and branches, usually covering each item with lichen.

In mixed Scots and Corsican pine plantations in East Anglia, J. A. Gibb found that both coal and willow tits preferred to hide their food under flakes of bark on dead branches or on the boles of pines, over 90 per cent of it 1–8 metres from the ground. Coal tits stored much pine seed, chiefly in spring, but in autumn also some aphids and insect larvae. Examination of gizzard contents of coal tits taken in the plantations in midwinter showed only a small proportion of stored food, though it included both pine seed and caterpillars.

Thus in the comparatively homogeneous habitats of the Caledonian Forest and East Anglian pine plantations British tits resemble Scandinavian ones in storing food in trees well above the ground and below the canopy, but differ from them in the fact that the different species show no specialisation in the parts of the tree used for storing. This difference might be partly due to the absence from the Caledonian Forest, at least in recent years, of the willow tit, which in Norway feeds chiefly on the trunks and main branches of trees, and to its comparative scarcity in English conifer plantations.

In broad-leaved and mixed woodland, parks and gardens the storing behaviour of tits is even less stereotyped than in British coniferous forests. Coal, marsh and willow tits will store food whenever there is a supply in excess of their immediate needs. Beech nuts from September to mid-December and pine seed in April and May are favourite items. Marsh tits hide yew seeds from September to May, and many other foods, including items from garden bird-tables, may be hoarded when they are locally abundant. Food-hiding is not limited to any particular season—I have records of it for the marsh tit in every month of the year and for the coal tit for every month except June—but it is most noticeable in spring and autumn and falls to a minimum in late winter, when food is presumably scarce, and in midsummer.

The distance between the source of the food and the hiding-place is extremely variable. I have seen coal tits repeatedly fly more than 180 metres to hide beech nuts, but they, unlike marsh tits, also hide many items close to their place of origin, even as near as 50 centimetres. The long-distance flights are sometimes apparently undertaken to escape pursuit by great and blue tits, which often follow coal tits over shorter distances and extract the hidden item while the 'owner' looks on with plaintive calls.

In these mixed habitats the actual sites of the caches are also varied and unpredictable. The marsh tit shows a more definite preference for the middle area of trees, which it also favours for food-searching, and it makes less use of evergreens than the coal tit, but otherwise the two species do not differ greatly in their choice of hiding places. Marsh tits hid food 2–8m above the ground in 37 per cent of my observations, coal tits in 24 per cent; marsh tits used evergreens only for 10 per cent of items, coal tits for 22 per cent. In trees favourite storage sites are behind stems of ivy, in crevices or behind flakes of bark, in the broken-off ends of small dead branches, or in dense matted twigs. In early December I watched one coal tit successfully fix a beech nut in an empty mast case 15 metres up in the parent tree. Where moss or lichen is easily available both coal and marsh tits will pull it briskly and efficiently over the hidden object, which is then difficult for the human eye to detect. Items stored on the ground are also carefully covered with grass, moss or dead leaves. Miscellaneous sites used by coal tits include tightly closed brassica leaves and bales of hay inside a dark, stone-built barn. Marsh tits have been seen to hide small black slugs in thick stems of dead plants.[15] One difference between the storing behaviour of the four regular hoarding species is that crested and coal tits only carry and hide one item of food at a time (except in the case of aphids, which are packed into a small ball), while marsh and willow tits will cram their bills with as many fragments of nut or other food as they can.

In view of the wide area over which the food is stored, the variety of hiding places used and the apparent unsuitability of some of them— food buried in the ground, for example, would be inaccessible under snow or hard frost—it is not likely that tits in broad-leaved woodland and gardens in the British Isles will recover any considerable quantity by the kind of random search that Haftorn believed to be effective in Norway. The proportion of items recovered would clearly be increased if the birds remembered the exact location of the food they had hidden, as nutcrackers and jays have been shown to do. It would be difficult to determine conclusively whether tits in the wild do or do not remember the sites of their food caches, but from personal observation I am convinced that both coal and marsh tits do so, sometimes at least. On several occasions I have seen them behaving in a way that could hardly be explained except by their having a precise idea of the site of a food store.

The usefulness of the ability to remember the site of a food cache must depend on the time that elapses between concealment and re-covery. A beech nut retrieved and eaten a few days after being hidden in November, when beech-mast is still plentiful, will be of much less value than one recovered in January or February. Many recoveries or losses are in fact short-term ones. Badly concealed items nearly always

Loose-feathered crown, pale secondaries and fine bill identify the willow tit shown here

Page 120   (*above*) A blue tit sets to work on a milk bottle; (*below*) confrontation between a blue tit and a great tit

disappear within a day or two, whether taken by the tit that hid them or by some other bird or mammal, and on several occasions a beech nut completely hidden under moss or other vegetation has remained for a few days but gone within a fortnight. One observer, Mrs J. Hall-Craggs, saw a coal tit (May 1959) dig up a seed which was almost certainly buried more than a fortnight before. An extreme example of short-term storing was observed by D. Hart, who found that a willow tit was taking 15–20 peanuts each morning from a bowl near his house and hiding them in the garden; when the bowl was empty it would begin searching for and eating the hidden peanuts.[16]

This kind of hiding gives the hoarder a certain advantage, as a coal, marsh or willow tit can hide at least 6 or 8 nuts in the time it takes a great or blue tit to eat one; and if, as in the case of the peanuts in the bowl, the supply is limited, food-hiding would be profitable even if half the items were lost. In fully natural conditions the usefulness of such storage is more doubtful. However, beech nuts collected from the ground and hidden in trees and walls are at least saved from competing species, including such large-scale consumers as woodpigeons and pheasants, and as nuts are only stored when the tits have both food and time to spare, any item recovered in time of need, whether by a feat of memory or by random search, represents some gain. Such a complex pattern of behaviour could hardly have developed if it did not bring some advantage to the species, but the storage methods do not appear to be fully adapted to present-day conditions in the British Isles and it seems unlikely that stored food makes a significant contribution to the survival of tits in winter in our gardens or in deciduous or mixed woodland.

8 Miscellaneous Activities

DAYTIME OCCUPATIONS

Even the most casual of birdwatchers must have noticed that big birds like swans, eagles and large gulls spend long periods of time in a state of passive inactivity while very small birds seem to be engaged in an almost continuous hunt for food. It has been estimated that in winter tits spend about 80 per cent of the daytime in feeding or searching for food, 5 per cent in preening, 5 per cent in resting and 10 per cent in miscellaneous activities.[1] J. A. Gibb found that in Marley Wood over a full year great tits fed for about 75 per cent of the day, blue tits for 85 per cent, coal tits 90 per cent and long-tailed tits 95 per cent. These figures accord with the general principle that the smaller the bird the greater its need for a very high rate of food intake.

The proportion of daylight hours spent in searching for food was also found to be highest in midwinter and again in early summer when the adults were feeding young; but even in winter tits find time for occasional preening. Preening must be considered almost as essential an activity as feeding, since a bird's survival depends on the maintenance of its plumage in good condition, the wing feathers for efficient flight and the body feathers for adequate insulation. Gibb saw great tits preening or resting in about 13 per cent of his observations, blue tits in 6 per cent, marsh tits in 5 per cent and coal tits in 4 per cent. Resting, for very brief spells in winter, often follows or interrupts a period of preening.

Preening, and the stereotyped movements by which it is carried out, are not peculiar to the tit family and are in fact common to nearly

all passerine species. Reproductive behaviour, taken to include territorial defence, song, display and inspection of nest-holes as well as
actual nest-building, incubation and care of the nestlings, takes up
much of the tits' available time in spring and early summer and has
been considered in Chapters 3, 4 and 5. So the first part of this chapter
is concerned with the more occasional leisure occupations of tits. These
miscellaneous activities are greatly influenced by weather conditions as
well as by seasonal changes.

One of the most striking examples of a bird's reaction to the weather
is sunbathing. Most birdwatchers will have observed blackbirds, song-
thrushes, starlings and perhaps other birds indulging in this curious
behaviour. The bird lies on the ground or some other flat surface in
hot sunshine with the tail and one or both wings spread out, the
feathers of head and body ruffled and the mandibles parted, and it may
remain in this posture for several minutes. In extreme cases the bird
seems to be almost in a state of trance and can be closely approached.
It is hardly necessary to stress the parallel with the condition of some
humans on holiday beaches.

This kind of high-intensity sunbathing is comparatively rare in the
tit family. The first published record of its occurrence in Britain was
that of T. S. Williams, who described the repeated sunbathing of two
juvenile great tits between 11 and 15 July 1945.[2] They 'lay motionless,
breast to ground, wings stretched out to the full and tail feathers
spread. The back feathers were puffed out and the whole body appeared
to be palpitating slowly.' This position was adopted for about a
minute at a time, after which the birds flew to a branch and began
preening. W. L. Colyer has given an interesting description of sunbathing by a family of 9 juvenile long-tailed tits, which sunned themselves together on the crown of a hawthorn tree with outspread wings
and tails, now and again vibrating their tail feathers.[3]

No other European tit is included in the list compiled by R. J.
Kennedy in 1969 of species which have been recorded sunbathing.[4] I
have personally seen full-intensity sunbathing by great tits twice: at
noon on 19 June 1960, by an adult which lay flat for about two
minutes on the dead branch of a tree with both wings and tail fully
spread, head on one side and bill gaping, and, briefly, by another adult
on the branch of a cherry tree against a wall, in July 1971. On 12 May

1971, a single adult marsh tit preened thoroughly in a hedge for about three minutes and then hopped down on to a small dead branch in full sun, where it lay with tail fully spread, left wing (on the sunny side) drooped over the branch, head slightly on one side and the feathers of the lower back and flank fluffed out. When a cloud came over the sun the marsh tit went up into the hedge, preened briefly and flew away.

In recent years there have been several published references to sun-bathing by great tits, though usually without great detail. The habit seems to have been regular among Len Howard's privileged and leisured birds. She describes one juvenile's striking deviation from nor-mal postures: it used to hang upside down from an exposed twig with spread wings and tail. But the fully developed form is not common among the other Paridae and may not occur at all in some of the smaller species.

The great tit, which has most often been seen sunbathing, takes larger food items than the other species and needs to hunt less con-tinuously, and it is also the species which most regularly feeds on the ground and might feel less insecure in exposed sunbathing positions. It may be significant that a young buzzard which I reared after it had fallen from a tree nest spent many hours sunbathing in attitudes of complete abandon on a lawn or a garden table, although the buzzard is not included in Kennedy's list of species with sunbathing records: it had abundant food without the need for hunting or begging, no fear, and flat warm surfaces available.

But although 'high-intensity' sunbathing may be unusual in the tit family varying degrees of less stereotyped sunning are not uncommon, especially in late summer. All the common British tits will sometimes preen on a perch in full sunshine with intermittent periods of resting with ruffled plumage. Adult and juvenile blue tits will often turn their backs to the sun with wings slightly drooped, the feathers of the rump and back fluffed out and sometimes the tail spread. Alternatively they turn their ruffled flank feathers towards the sun and lean away from it, with one foot drawn up into the abdominal feathers and sometimes with the neck stretched out in an abnormal attitude. This posture is chiefly used by great tits, sometimes by blue tits. I have seen five or six mixed great and blue tits preening and sunning like this in the same tree on three successive July afternoons.

In discussing the possible functions of sunbathing in birds D. Goodwin distinguished high-intensity sunbathing from sunning 'simply to get warm'.[5] My own impression is that the difference between high-intensity sunbathing and simple sunning in tits is one of degree rather than of kind. If the bird is undisturbed simple sunning may progress to sunbathing in the more specialised postures described above; and there is every indication that all forms of sunbathing or sunning by tits are motivated by enjoyment of the sensation of warmth. This seems to be a basic sensual pleasure common to many forms of life from butterflies and lizards to foxes, cats and man. Birds in fact show every sign of enjoying warmth for its own sake: for example, an injured blue tit kept at liberty in a London flat used to hop inside the shade of a reading lamp as soon as the light was switched on and became so addicted to this artificial sunbathing that it actually singed its feathers on the bulb.[6]

However, this does not exclude the possibility that sunbathing has some additional function. It has been argued that in its more extreme forms this habit must expose a bird to considerable danger from predators, so that it would have been eliminated by natural selection if it did not provide some positive benefit to compensate for the risk. A theory frequently repeated is that exposure to the sun produces vitamin D in the preen oil, and that some of this is ingested by the bird when preening or is absorbed through the skin. But R. J. Kennedy claimed there was no definite proof that vitamin D is obtained in this way, and if sunbathing were a reaction to a deficiency of this vitamin, one would expect it to occur most frequently in early spring, whereas in my experience it is far more common in all species from midsummer to autumn and may be repeated day after day in sunny summer weather. Other possibilities are that sunbathing stimulates external parasites into activity and makes them easier for the bird to remove, that it facilitates the moult in some way, and that it stimulates the action of the preen gland. None of these has been proved.

'Anting' is a somewhat similar pattern of behaviour adopted by some birds. In the passive form of anting a bird lies on the ground and allows ants to run up its outspread wings and tail into its plumage; in the active form the bird picks up ants and rubs them on the underside of its wings and tail. On three occasions blue tits have been observed using the active form of anting, which may help to remove parasites or improve the condition of the plumage, but these seem to be the only published records of such behaviour by any of the tits.[7]

The tits, like most other small birds, not infrequently bathe in shallow standing water, and when heavy rain follows a period of drought or frost there is often a burst of bathing activity in the puddles on roadways and other hard surfaces. At other times they use any water that may be available, including the pools formed in the forks of large trees. The bathing movements of tits are similar to those of many other passerine genera and consist of two main components which often alternate with each other. In one the bird stands or crouches in shallow water with ruffled plumage and dips the head and neck under the surface, simultaneously flicking both wings in the air. In the other it stands much more erect with the tail in the water and rapidly flicks the wings, thus sending out a spray which effectively wets its lower back. Juvenile tits are obviously puzzled by standing water when they first meet it, but once they have touched and tasted it their bathing and drinking actions are instinctive.

Bathing presumably helps to keep the feathers in good condition, though it is not clear exactly how it does this. Washing in the ordinary sense does not seem to be a major consideration, as tits will bathe as readily in dirty and discoloured water as in a clear spring. The net result is a controlled wetting of the plumage, sometimes thorough enough to make the bird's flight laboured and slow. Normally bathing is followed, after some preliminary shaking to remove surplus water, by prolonged preening, head-scratching and sometimes sunning.

Although the normal bathing actions of passerine birds are so stereotyped that they can be classified as 'fixed action patterns', tits sometimes adapt themselves to circumstances and wet their plumage by highly individual and unorthodox methods. Mrs D. Knappett reports that at about 5.30 on a fine sunny morning in May or June 1956 she and her husband found a coal tit splashing on the water in a little pool, some 50 centimetres across, in a stream in their garden in the Lake District. It swam, or rowed itself with its wings, to the bank near the observers and climbed out. Then it deliberately hopped back into the water and progressed in the same manner, beating the surface with both wings, across the pool to the other side. The bird's plumage was then so waterlogged that it could not fly, so Mrs Knappett picked it up and put it on a branch. There it shook itself and began a thorough preening.

Birds of a few passerine species, including blue and great tits, have been seen to bathe in wet foliage. In June 1971 Miss N. H. Butterworth saw a blue tit ducking into wet grass in her garden with typical bathing movements; another blue tit twice flew down and attacked it but then began to bathe in the same way. The neighbouring bird-bath was occupied by a blackbird and a starling at the time, but both blue and great tits have been seen to bathe in wet grass and foliage even when a garden pool was available nearby.[8] In February 1972 Miss Butterworth watched a blue tit in an evergreen shrub repeatedly slide down the decurving leaves and twigs, which were covered with damp snow, until its underparts were very wet. It then flew off and preened. A great tit has been seen to draw itself by its feet slowly up a wet tea-cloth on a clothes line with its body pressed close to the damp surface. On reaching the top it flew down to repeat the whole operation from bottom to top and then preened on the line.[9]

Both great and blue tits have also been observed snow-bathing. W. D. Clague describes one of the latter 'having a snow-bath in much the same way as a bird would take a dust bath.[10] The snow was dry and powdery and about two inches deep.' Bathing continued for about a minute and a half. I have only seen an incomplete form of snow-bathing in which a blue tit stood for a few seconds in shallow dry snow flicking its wings and sending out a shower of powdery snow. This is a typical water-bathing action. Dust-bathing involves a different set of movements with the bird lying down on the ground, and is commonly seen in gallinaceous birds and in larks and house-sparrows, but very few other passerine genera. Ida Smith wrote that the actions of a blue tit she watched in powdery snow were 'a combination of those of dusting and water-bathing.[11] It first wriggled its body into the snow, then pushed its head under and jerked it up to throw snow over its back and half-spread, fluttering wings.' It repeated this several times. During the exceptional irruption of tits in the autumn of 1957 there were many instances of tits entering houses, and one blue tit was reported to have taken a dust-bath in a powder-bowl on a dressing-table, a nice example of ready opportunism in the care of skin and feathers! Indeed, it appears that blue tits are exceptionally adaptable and can use either of two different and generally stereotyped patterns of action in response to powdery substances, or may combine movements derived from each of them.

Although tits give every indication of enjoying deliberately wetting their plumage, they apparently try to escape the wetting effect of prolonged heavy rain, which seems to leave them with bedraggled head and body feathers. On several occasions I have seen great and blue tits resting close to the trunk of dense evergreens during heavy rain. For example, on 7 August 1970 three blue tits were feeding in rose bushes in my garden when heavy thundery rain suddenly began to fall. All three immediately flew up into a nearby yew tree and rested there for several minutes. Two flew off when the rain slackened but the third sat almost motionless for fifteen minutes until the shower passed. R. J. Kennedy refers to a report of a blue tit sheltering from rain under a large leaf.[12]

Activity at garden feeding-stations is also greatly reduced during short periods of heavy precipitation, although during very prolonged rain feeding seems to return almost to normal, presumably through compulsion by hunger. In high winds tits avoid tree tops and other exposed positions.

One other feature of tit behaviour should be mentioned here, the searching, pecking, tapping and tearing that is particularly noticeable among young birds in late summer and autumn. Some at least of these actions do not appear to be directly concerned with finding food but may be a form of exploration and discovery, or even play. This kind of activity will be discussed in Chapter 11.

ROOSTING

A description of roosting habits may seem out of place under the heading of 'activities', but as tits spend roughly half their lives asleep it is a subject that should not be ignored. Moreover, as was shown in Chapter 3, the business of going to roost is far from inactive during courtship, and in the period from midsummer to early spring with which this chapter is chiefly concerned the finding of adequate shelter and security for the night must be of great importance. Tits are much more careful not to be seen entering a roosting-hole than a nesting-hole, and some individuals are equally cautious about leaving the roost in the morning. I have seen one suspicious great tit remain motionless looking out of its hole for forty seconds before flying off. As some tits use the same roost-hole regularly for long periods, and as they are inevitably vulnerable to predators such as weasels at night, this caution is obviously valuable.

The same caution may partly account for the scanty information available about the roosting habits of the crested tit and the willow tit in the British Isles. Both species are adept at disappearing from view as dusk approaches.

For three or four months after leaving the nest, young great, blue and marsh tits and the great majority of adults normally roost in dense vegetation of some kind, and the same is probably true of coal tits. R. A. Hinde found that great and blue tits in Marley Wood usually roosted in dense hawthorn, hazel and elder, showing a marked preference for certain parts of the wood. Elsewhere, ivy on tree-trunks or walls was favoured at this time of year, and also rhododendrons and other thick bushes and hedges. Major R. F. Ruttledge found ivy the commonest site for coal tits in Ireland.[13] Long-tailed tits continue to roost in vegetation throughout the winter and parties of five to ten of these birds have been seen packed together, presumably for warmth, on a single branch or twig, or huddled into a ball in a thicket.

However, between September and December the *Parus* tits change their roosting behaviour, and throughout the winter and spring most of them habitually sleep in holes or crevices in trees. The change is not in fact due to the lack of concealment in deciduous hedges and bushes as the leaves fall, since many of the tits have been roosting in evergreens. There is no obvious reason why the improved security from predators afforded by a small hole should be of greater importance in winter than in late summer, so it seems likely that warmth, and protection from wind and rain, is the chief consideration. It is perhaps surprising that the *Parus* tits roost singly even in the coldest weather and never huddle together for warmth. Like most passerine birds they conserve heat by fluffing out their plumage, as far as the site permits, and normally sleep with the bill buried in the scapulars, not tucked underneath the wing.

A wide variety of holes is used for roosting, but both blue and great tits seem to prefer a small cavity that they can only just squeeze into.

Favourite natural sites for great, blue and marsh tits in my own district are the crevices in the trunks of old yew trees. One April a great tit continued to sleep night after night in one of these cracks although a wren was filling it up with nest material during the day. Some of the crevices are so constricted that the tits roosting in them acquire conspicuously bent tails. In Berkshire, blue tits quite frequently roosted in shallow holes caused by the rotting away of branches, about 5cm deep and 2·5–4·5m up the trunk.[14] Coal tits are sometimes found sleeping in cavities (usually 5–7cm deep and about 5cm in diameter) in soft rotten tree trunks, especially Scots pine and ash. Some of these holes are no doubt originally excavated by treecreepers, like the well-known ones in the soft bark of wellingtonias *Sequoia gigantea*, but others are apparently made by the tits themselves. Coal tits also sometimes roost in old nests of other birds, especially those of the thrush family.

In an urban environment blue tits may roost in man-made holes hardly less eccentric than some of their nest-sites. Street lamps have been used in several districts: 19 out of 34 sodium discharge lamps in Salisbury were occupied by blue tits in October 1959, and occasional great tits were also found in them.[15] One can understand the attraction for tits of a centrally heated dormitory, but the choice of one that is also brightly illuminated is surprising. Len Howard had her tame blue and great tits sleeping on a picture rail and later in boxes attached to the wall of her bedroom. There was sometimes fierce competition for the possession of a particular box, but tits will roost peacefully in separate holes in close proximity. R. A. Hinde found one tree in Marley Wood occupied by several great and blue tits as well as two great spotted woodpeckers and one or two nuthatches.

Roosting in nest-boxes is common, and in some woodlands such as young conifer plantations where there are few natural holes, nearly all the great and blue tits will roost in them. H. M. Kluijver was able to estimate the winter population of great tits in certain Dutch woods from the number of boxes occupied by roosting birds. But when natural holes and crevices are available nest-boxes are not so often used, perhaps because the interior space is so much bigger than that of normal roosting-holes. I have never found more than 8 of my 25 local boxes occupied on any one night, although over 20 of them have been used for nesting in each of the last five years. However, the numbers of occupied boxes found in monthly visits in 1969–70 confirmed the increase in hole-roosting towards midwinter: 1 July, 1 August, 3 October, 5 November, 5 December, 8 January, 7 February, 6 March. On average there were twice as many great tits as blue tits.

Both in boxes and natural sites tits prefer to roost well above ground level. Great and blue tits in my boxes nearly always chose those 2m up the tree trunks and rarely used the low ones. The average height of 20 coal tit roosts in Ireland was 3m, with a maximum of 6·5m, and marsh tits in Bagley Wood roosted in the hollow ends of branches between 3 and 9m up the tree.

Individual birds vary in their fidelity to particular roosting sites. Most marsh and many coal tits change roosts frequently, blue and great tits less so. For two successive winters the same female (colour-ringed) blue tit regularly retired to roost under the same slate in the roof of my house, and a blue tit has been observed to roost for three winters in succession on a perch in an inverted cream carton hung close to a window.[16] This site is so unusual that the occupant may be presumed to have been the same bird each year.

Tits retire to roost earlier in the evening and rise later in the morning than most woodland birds. On summer evenings warblers and fly-catchers are still active for a quarter of an hour or more after the last blue or great tit has settled for the night, and throughout the year blackbirds, thrushes and robins are consistently later than any of the tits in going to roost and are earlier about in the morning. Differences between the *Parus* species themselves in their roosting times tend to be masked by variations between individuals and also of the same bird, but on average great tits go to roost several minutes earlier than blue tits. The fact that the great tit has a shorter active day has been at-tributed to the fact that a bigger bird does not need to feed as frequently as a smaller one and has less difficulty in maintaining its body tem-perature through a winter night. It has been shown experimentally that a great tit provided with peanuts all day roosted on average thirteen minutes earlier than on days when no extra food was provided.[17]

However, the coal tit, the smallest species, seems to be a variable but generally early rooster. Three coal tits watched by Major Ruttledge on ten days in December and January averaged 1·7 minutes before local sunset. D. J. May found one in Surrey regularly in its roost half an hour before sunset in February,[18] and at a Hampshire bird-table G. Marples recorded the last coal tit 15 minutes before sunset, half an hour earlier than the last great tit.[19] On the other hand, two Irish coal tits averaged 24 minutes after sunset on six evenings in October. Marsh tits generally seem to roost about the same time as blue tits, or a little later. In all species the male of a mated pair normally rises shortly before the female and goes to roost several minutes later. If the early times given above for coal tits are typical, the usual order of going to roost in winter is: coal tit, great tit, blue tit and/or marsh tit. This order cannot be linked in any way with body size.

Although the times of roosting and rising are obviously related to the times of sunset and sunrise through the year, the relationship is not a simple one. In late summer tits go to roost in broad daylight, an hour or more before local sunset, whereas in midwinter they are active till dusk and most species retire several minutes after sunset. In winter all the available daylight hours are needed for the search for food, but there is not the same pressure in the (probable) greater abundance and longer days of summer. R. A. Hinde found that near Oxford great tits went to roost on average 1 minute after sunset in November, 5 minutes after in December, and 5, 12 and 16 minutes before sunset in January, February and March respectively. Blue tits in the Oxford woods showed a similar trend but went to roost 'a few minutes later'.

In north-west England, midwinter roosting times seem to be considerably later. Two blue tits averaged 19·5 minutes after sunset on 18 dates in December and January, and a great tit 12 minutes after sunset on three dates in January. These times are not in any way exceptional: great, blue and marsh tits are regularly active well after local sunset from November to March inclusive. Crested and coal tits on Speyside were still feeding 9 and 14 minutes respectively after local sunset as early as 22 October. These times suggest that later roosting in the north of Britain may be compensating for shorter day-length in winter. (On 1 January the period from sunrise to sunset in London is 20 minutes longer than in Manchester and 39 minutes longer than in Glasgow.)

However, G. Marples's observations of feeding times on the south coast of England show that even there some tits go to roost much later than those studied by Professor Hinde in Marley Wood. In January, Marples's last great tits averaged 7·6 minutes after local sunset and blue tits 24 minutes after, and in March, 4 and 16·7 minutes after sunset respectively. It would be interesting to collect and compare average roosting times from other parts of the British Isles.

There is much less seasonal and regional variation in the time of leaving the roost in the morning in relation to sunrise, and less difference between the species. R. A. Hinde found little change from December to March in the relative rising times of great tits, the average being about 20 minutes before sunrise; blue tits were slightly earlier. In Westmorland in midwinter the first appearance of great tits averaged 21 minutes before local sunrise, blue tits 22·5 minutes, and in Hampshire great tits averaged 10 minutes before sunrise, blue tits 16·9 minutes. In December and January, Irish coal tits rose on average 24 minutes before sunrise.

Both Kluijver and Hinde emphasised that in winter the light intensity is much lower when great tits rise in the morning than when they go to roost in the evening, but this is not always so in the north of England. It is often difficult to see blue and great tits in the dusk when they finally slip into the roost-hole. Several observers have noticed a tendency for tits to retire to roost earlier on dull overcast evenings than on clear ones, and there is little doubt that light intensity is one of the factors influencing roosting times. But it is certainly not the only one. Hunger or local disturbance may delay roosting. Heavy rain or snow tends to induce earlier roosting and later emergence in the morning.

9 *Individuality and Intelligence*

Every dog-owner knows that no two dogs are alike in temperament or intelligence, and keepers of other mammals, from elephants to white mice, would say the same of their charges. Acceptance of the fact that there may be similar differences between wild birds of the same species has probably been delayed by the difficulty of recognising individuals in the field. It does indeed require an effort of the imagination to look at a flock of thousands of starlings gathering to roost, or dunlins performing their intricate co-ordinated flights over the mudbanks, and think of them as individuals, each with a character of its own. Yet among the tits it is certainly true that particular birds of each species differ widely in their aggressiveness, tolerance or timidity in relation to other birds, in their confidence and tameness with humans, in their food preferences, in the variety of their vocal utterances, in their choice of nest sites and materials, in their diligence and devotion as parents, and in many other respects. Some great and blue tits also show surprising originality and adaptability in feeding, bathing, display and other activities.

In order to study these differences it is of course essential to be able to recognise individual birds with certainty, and there are two effective ways of doing this. One is to win the birds' confidence to such an extent that they will readily feed from the hand, so that minute differences of build, plumage and mannerism can be distinguished. This method was developed to an extraordinary degree by Miss Len Howard, who achieved a remarkable mutual understanding with great tits, as she describes in full detail in her books *Birds as Individuals* and *Living with*

134

Birds. However, few birdwatchers will have the time, the patience or perhaps the special talent necessary to achieve results like this, and it must be admitted that for free birds to live in such close association with and dependence upon a human being is so unusual that their behaviour may be considered to some extent abnormal.

The other method is to catch the tits one is studying and mark them individually with coloured plastic rings on the tarsus of one or both legs. The ringed birds can then be identified with binoculars up to a range of 20 metres or more. The chief disadvantage of this method is that a bird tends to behave in a nervous and unnatural manner for some days after it has been trapped and handled and may even be frightened away from the scene of its experience. Also the number of blue tits visiting a garden during a single winter may be so large that one is obliged to use combinations of barred or striped rings that become difficult to differentiate when the bird is moving about in a tree. A second year's ringing programme is impracticable in these circumstances, although it is possible to continue marking the less abundant species for several years in succession. Readers should note, however, that a licence must be obtained from the Nature Conservancy Council for the trapping and marking of birds, and a permit from the British Trust for Ornithology is also required so as to avoid the possibility of confusion if two or more people should be using coloured rings in the same district.

When several colour-ringed tits feed regularly at the same place, certain differences between them in behaviour and temperament soon become apparent. The most striking is the degree of confidence and dominance shown towards other birds, especially those of their own species. One or two individual great and blue tits appear to establish proprietorial rights at the bird-table or nut-basket, and their claims are recognised and accepted by the other tits. The dominant birds are regular attenders, and it soon becomes clear that they are permanent residents in the neighbourhood of the feeding place. Anne Brian studied the relationship between half a dozen pairs of great tits at a feeding-station and found that the order of precedence among them depended upon the distance between the food supply and their respective territories, the nearer birds being fairly consistently superior to the more distant ones.[1] M. K. Colquhoun recorded a similar situation with blue tits.[2] Male great tits nearly always dominated females, but when two females met their status normally corresponded with that of their respective mates.

This suggests that the apparent differences in behaviour between tits at a feeding station are due to external circumstances rather than to their individual temperaments, but in fact this is only partly true. Within the general pattern of the influence of territory on dominance there are still considerable differences between individual birds in disposition and attitude towards others. My own feeding-station is practically equidistant from two nest-boxes occupied by colour-ringed blue tits, and for nearly two years it was completely dominated by the male from one of them, 'Mr P', while the pair from the other box were a peaceful and tolerant couple who often fed amicably with other tits. Other blue tits nearly always fled when 'Mr P' arrived, or they waited till he had finished feeding before attempting to do so themselves. Both male and female great tits also gave way to him, and the only defeat I saw him suffer was from a greenfinch which bit his foot when he tried to kick it off the nut-basket. 'Mr P' disappeared on 21 February 1972, probably the victim of a local sparrowhawk and his own incautious habit of singing conspicuously from the topmost twig of his nest-box tree. By 26 February his widow was associating with a new mate, unringed but recognisable by his pale dishevelled crown. Compared with his ebullient predecessor the second husband was a retiring and colourless character. Although his timidity may at first have been due to the novelty of his position, he became only moderately more confident with time: he rarely sang and showed little hostility to other tits at the feeding-station. Len Howard gives numerous examples of wide differences in personality, apparently quite unrelated to territory, among her great tits.

One of the striking features of the established order of dominance among tits at a feeding place is the ease and quickness with which the birds seem to recognise each other. When 'Mrs P' joined her first mate on the nut-basket he always accepted her without even looking up. The swift response of other blue tits to his arrival could have been due to his confident, aggressive manner of approach, but when they found him already feeding they must have recognised him as an individual. One cannot know how many of the tits visiting a feeding place come to be individually recognised in this way, but normally there seems to be a nucleus of regular attenders with an acknowledged position, while casual visitors tend to be nervous and lacking in confidence. When Averil Morley was baiting marsh tits in Bagley Wood, she observed a marked contrast between the confident behaviour of the resident pair and the guilty timidity of trespassing territory-owners, while landless birds from a flock were subordinate to the territory-owners but were tolerated by them. She reported that the marsh tit can not only recognise its mate but also 'its neighbours, whom it can pick out in the flock, and apparently distinguish from the subordinate flock marsh tits, up to a distance of 60 yards (55m) at least.'

In normal circumstances the tits show a fear or distrust of humans that could be innate: nestlings will crouch and shrink away from a human face soon after their eyes are open, even when there are no warning calls from watching parents, though this may be a generalised reaction to any disturbance. In many cases this caution will be reinforced by parental alarm at the approach of humans during the fortnight or so after the young leave the nest, and one can rarely tell whether subsequent differences between individual tits in tameness are due to previous experience or to temperament and disposition.

It is interesting that the tameness of birds, including the tits, is often associated with particular places rather than with particular people. Popular picnic sites or certain parts of public parks attract a regular clientèle of avian mendicants, often including at least three of the *Parus* tits as well as nuthatches, chaffinches and other species. At some of these sites the birds will feed from the hand. Four species of tits do this at Toys Hill near Westerham, Kent, and near Tatton Park in Cheshire. (Yet many householders must have been surprised by the slowness of tits to notice or recognise food put out for them only a few metres from the usual site.) At these special places all humans appear to be accepted without distinction as benevolent, provided that they are reasonably quiet and slow in their movements. But this does not mean that tits are unable to recognise individual people. Averil Morley's marsh tits in Bagley Wood followed anyone, male or female, who approached the feeding places, but on one occasion they greeted her on a road on the edge of the wood, although several other pedestrians were passing at the time. Great tits recognised Len Howard across two fields even when she was wearing unfamiliar clothing, and there is no doubt that in her case the birds were attached primarily to her as a person and not simply as the occupant of a regular feeding place, as they would fly to meet her even in other people's gardens. One great tit resumed its familiar relationship at once after an absence of two years, a considerable feat of memory. Others were hesitant after only a few weeks.

Some of the differences between individual tits in 'character' and emotional reactions may well be due to differences in glandular activity and the stage of the annual reproductive cycle that they have reached, but it seems likely that sometimes more permanent factors are involved, some of which may be hereditary. The differences between individual tits in 'intelligence', or the ability to learn from experience and find the solution to a problem, are presumably of this kind, and they are even more striking than the differences in disposition or emotional make-up that have been mentioned so far in this chapter. Professor W. H. Thorpe has defined learning as 'the production of adaptive changes in individual behaviour as a result of experience', as contrasted with innate or instinctive behaviour 'which appears at the appropriate time in the individual life cycle irrespective of special experience'.[3] Tits, with their highly developed exploratory instinct, probably acquire a greater variety of habits through 'trial-and-error learning' than most groups of birds. This is shown in the very wide range of their diet, for the edibility or otherwise of each item has to be learnt by experience, and in the adaptability of their feeding methods and postures. However, this kind of learning by accidental discovery is often slow. E. J. M. Buxton found that after the war great tits took nearly a month to learn that the kernels of peanuts inside the husk were edible and could be extracted, even though the birds were helped by the removal of part of the shell.[4] When two or three great tits were eventually successful blue and coal tits still failed to follow their example.

A type of behaviour that is of special interest in relation to the tit family is 'insight learning', defined by Professor Thorpe as 'sudden adaptive re-organisation of experience', or 'the sudden production of a new adaptive response not arrived at by overt trial-and-error behaviour'. Briefly, this is the kind of action that in everyday usage would be called 'intelligent', showing a grasp of the nature of a problem and a direct way to its solution, without trial-and-error discovery. A classic example of insight learning is the use by caged chimpanzees of a bamboo pole to bring down inaccessible fruit, as this involves the employment of a primitive form of tool. The existence of this kind of insight in birds has been doubted, but some great and blue tits, and occasional individuals of other *Parus* species, have been known to achieve quick solutions to certain problems in ways that seemed to show a real understanding of the situation and gave no hint of accidental trial-and-error discovery. Great tits for example have been seen to obtain food at garden feeding-stations by pulling up the string on which it was suspended and holding the loops on the perch with one or both feet. Individuals of other species, including some of the corvids, finches and a house-sparrow, have behaved in the same way.

In my own garden I tried sundry baits on varying lengths and thicknesses of string and thread but never saw any bird try to pull up the string. Great, blue, coal and marsh tits all hung on the bait itself while feeding on it. Great tits would hang on by one foot even when only half a peanut was left. However, when the bait was suspended by a string inside a glass jar the reactions of the different great and blue tits were remarkably varied (Fig 1). The resident male great tit, 'yellow left', pulled up the brazil nut by the string without any hesitation, held it up by clasping the two loops under his feet and began to feed. He was seen to obtain food successfully in the same way six times during tests on seven days: there were no unsuccessful attempts. Subsequently he sometimes used the same string-pulling method to reach suspended nuts after the jar was removed. His mate once managed to reach down and pull up the bait itself, but she never attempted to use the string.

A female blue tit, 'Mrs A', from a neighbouring nest-box, raised the bait by pulling in two loops of string at her first visit; on later occasions she used as many as four loops on a longer string. Her mate was apparently baffled by the problem and reacted by driving his wife off the jar. However, on the fourth day of the experiment he watched Mrs A pull up the cheese and feed, then took her place and began to pull up the string. He succeeded at the third attempt and fed. But when he returned an hour later he twice perched on the rim of the jar and looked down at the bait with raised crest and once fluttered round it

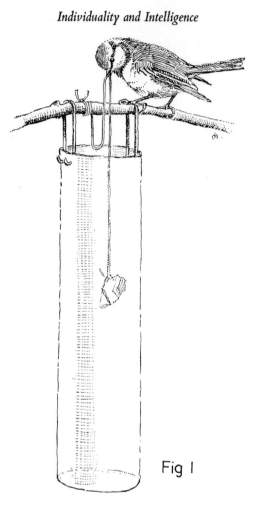

Fig I

pecking at the glass, but made no attempt then or later to use the string. There has been considerable doubt whether birds ever do actually imitate the actions of others,[5] and there are certainly many occasions when their failure to do so is so conspicuous as to be positively exasperating to the observer, but this incident gave the impression that the male blue tit was copying the female's actions without any real insight into their purpose.

Two other blue tits succeeded in solving the problem of the hanging bait in the jar. The dominant male, Mr P, at first fluttered round the jar, but he too watched Mrs A pull up the bait, drove her off and used the same method successfully himself. He had three subsequent successes and no failures. On the seventh day of the test an unringed adult blue tit succeeded in raising the bait and feeding at the fourth attempt, after spending about 2½ minutes on the jar or the branch above. At least four other blue tits studied the jar but failed to solve the problem.

It has been suggested that string-pulling may be attributed to an innate pattern of action used by some tits and finches when feeding on catkins, but although I have seen blue tits pull up and hold birch catkins in this way tits more often hang from the catkin itself when feeding. The examples above show that this loop-pulling was only used to deal with a new situation when the normal 'hanging-on' was impossible. The string appeared to be used consciously as a kind of tool to raise the food. It is said that blue tits have been seen to pull up caterpillars by the silk threads on which they were descending from leaves, but this seems to be exceptional and there is nothing to suggest that it is a regular or instinctive feeding method.

In experiments with twelve wild great tits in an aviary it was found that only one pulled up sunflower seeds suspended inside a glass cylinder on a 10cm string, but four others were 'trained' to do so by starting with a very short string and gradually increasing the length.[6] Even successful birds lost the habit temporarily when aviary conditions were altered, presumably because of lack of concentration due to fear or other distractions. Juvenile tits have been shown to be generally more successful than fully adult birds: this may be explained by their stronger exploratory urge. Success depends partly on the degree of interest or appetite shown by the individual bird, but the fact that some find a solution more quickly than others does not necessarily exclude 'insight learning' as the true explanation of most of the successful operations. It is possible, however, that the trained birds discovered the use of string to raise the food by the trial-and-error method.

In the simple tests described above, the nut or cheese, the reward for solving the problem, was clearly visible, but M. Brooks-King devised a series of more difficult puzzles in which the nuts could only just be seen.[7] In an early test with a wooden cylinder the nut was obtained by pulling a string and the problem was quickly solved by at least one blue tit and one great tit. Then an entirely different apparatus was set up, consisting of a vertical matchbox with the lower half of the front cut away, and a piece of bent card fitted into the empty inner box in

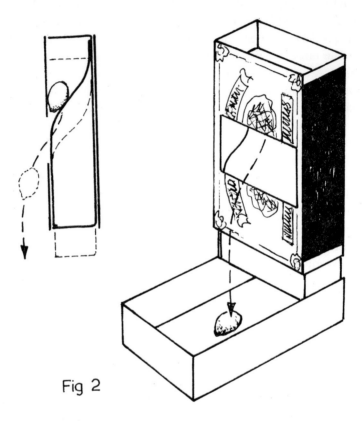

Fig 2

such a way that a smart tap on the top of it would release a peanut into a tray below (Fig 2). A male great tit, in trying to excavate the nut from several points, started pecking at the top of the inner box and so knocked it down and obtained his reward. On every subsequent visit he went straight to the top of the box and tapped until the nut dropped. No other tit solved the problem at that time, but when the test was repeated in 1955 a female blue tit was successful almost at once, while her mate took three months to achieve a correct solution. (Ardent feminists should not conclude from one or two examples that all female blue tits are more intelligent than males, but it would help to maintain a balance of numbers between the sexes if females, which are often driven off food by aggressive males, showed greater resourcefulness in obtaining it.) Successful birds never relapsed, and they remembered the correct method of operation even after the apparatus was removed for eight weeks. 'When the box was closed the nut was only just visible through the hole in the cover, when looking upward from immediately below', and it was suggested that the tits might have detected it by a keen sense of smell. However, from the evidence to be given in Chapter 11 it seems unlikely that tits locate food by smell. An alternative possibility is that these tits had come to regard any new apparatus in this particular place as a possible food container and so worth a thorough exploratory search.

In 1955 a further series of matchbox tests was devised in which the reward was obtained by pulling open a drawer, removing pegs, pulling a string, or a combination of these actions. The original female blue tit solved all these problems and apparently some other tits were also successful. They also learnt to operate a vertical revolving disc with projecting perches and an attached test-tube which dropped a nut into a tray if the bird alighted on the correct perch (Fig 3). This of course involved an entirely different method of obtaining the reward, involving a considerable descent on a moving perch. H. G. Hurrell had one blue tit which pulled a truck up an incline to obtain its reward.[8] He also tried out a new apparatus consisting of two vertical sheets of Perspex about 12mm apart with rows of matchsticks inserted through corresponding holes in each sheet, so as to support peanuts at various heights. If a bird pulled out a stick the peanut above it dropped down to the next level and eventually came out in a tray at the bottom. In a series of thirty tests, blue tits succeeded in obtaining 63 nuts and coal tits 14. Great tits were present during every test and marsh tits in eight of them but neither species succeeded in extracting a nut, though great tits sometimes robbed successful blue tits. It was not known how many blue and coal tits were successful, but the achievement of one coal tit which dropped a peanut from top to bottom of the apparatus through five stages without making a single mistake was particularly noteworthy. This performance seems to suggest insight into the nature of the problem rather than random experimentation, but the tests with matchboxes and the revolving disc must have been solved by trial-and-

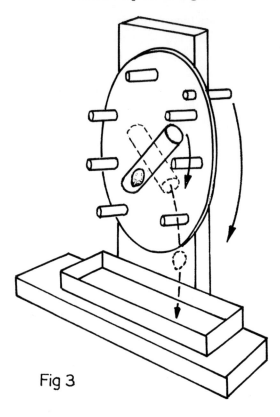

Fig 3

error methods. Nevertheless, the speed and efficiency with which the problems were tackled by some of the tits were striking. The experimenters were impressed by the varying ability and persistence of the birds, the keenness shown by some in exploiting their success and their retentive memory for a correct solution. H. G. Hurrell made a fascinating film of some of the tits at work on the puzzles, and his performers have received the accolade of appearance on the television screen.

W. H. Thorpe investigated two examples of blue tits showing even more extraordinary ingenuity in obtaining food.[9] In 1938 Mr Trevor Miller of Riding Mill, Northumberland, put up a conical, smooth-sided tit-bell half filled with fat. A fine string about 10cm long was hung centrally through the fat and a light stick of balsa wood was tied firmly by its middle to the end of the string (Fig 4). On the second day after this apparatus was put up, one or more blue tits, unable to reach the fat in any other way, alighted on the balsa stick and, hanging upside down, rolled the bar up the thread with rapid movements of the feet and so arrived at the food. This process was observed once or twice a day for several weeks; but although the experiment was tried again in subsequent years and in other places there was no repetition of this astonishing feat.

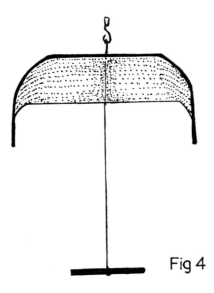

Fig 4

In 1956 Mr S. Anderson had an inverted coconut shell containing fat hanging up in his garden near Thame, Oxfordshire. A wooden bar was suspended below the nutshell by a string at each end. When most of the fat had been pecked away, so that it was difficult or impossible for the birds to reach the remainder, a blue tit alighted on the perch 'and suddenly proceeded to twist it up the string till the bar contacted the rim of the shell. Always its claws moved so fast that one could hardly see their movement.' The habit continued for a period of some weeks and it was almost certain that more than one blue tit was feeding in this way.

It is hardly credible that the tits could have 'thought out' these difficult manoeuvres by 'insight learning', but at the very least they showed a remarkable skill and ingenuity in exploiting an accidental discovery. They presumably found that certain movements of the feet brought them a little nearer their objective and then persevered till they reached it. If more than one bird was using the perch-rolling method in either place it must surely have been due to imitation: it is highly improbable that two birds would independently hit upon the same extraordinary solution to the problem at the same time and in the same place.

This brief catalogue of the more outstanding accomplishments of tits would not be complete without some reference to the achievements of Len Howard's mathematical great tit, 'Star', as described in *Living with Birds*. 'Star' was a female, already six or seven years old when Miss Howard began to teach her to reply to pencil taps on a table with the same number of taps with her beak. In ten days she graduated from two taps to six. Once, when given six taps she answered with five, began to fly for her nut, the customary reward, but turned back, gave one more tap and then returned for the nut. Four weeks later she answered eight beats correctly, with a slight pause after the first four. After a spring and summer interval tapping was resumed and again numbers up to and including eight were answered correctly. The following winter, correct responses were given in varying rhythms, for instance six as 3,3 or 2,2,2 or 4,2. Miss Howard then began giving spoken instructions, at first accompanied by pencil taps, then with the spoken word alone. At first 'Star' had difficulty with the words 'five' and 'seven', but when these were clearly enunciated as 'fife' and 'sept' she answered correctly, again in varying rhythms. Miss Howard writes that 'Star' sometimes refused to tap at all, but if she did respond her answers, with a very few specified exceptions, were always correct. She never succeeded with the number nine, as she always started to tap her answer before the nine was completed. No other tit achieved any correct answer. 'Star' disappeared in the April following her success with spoken instructions.

Controlled experiments with other birds have shown that ravens, parrots and especially jackdaws can solve certain problems which involve 'thinking unnamed numbers', usually not higher than six, and some birds have responded to instructions with spoken numbers,[9] but

'Star's' achievements were perhaps more impressive than any of these. A possible explanation is that great tits probably have a very keen ear for rhythm and for patterns of sound. The commonest form of song consists of the repetition of two notes up to eight times, and male great tits recognise and reply to the songs of their neighbours. Some individuals practise vocal mimicry. So 'Star' was, in effect, doing instrumentally what cock great tits sometimes do vocally 'in the wild'.

However, some of 'Star's' successes could have been of the 'Clever Hans' type. Clever Hans was a remarkable stallion who could tap out with his hoof the correct answers to abstruse mathematical problems. But it was eventually found that Hans only gave the correct answer when it was also known to the questioner, and that he was in fact responding to slight involuntary movements made unknowingly by the trainer when the horse had given the right number of taps. Miss Howard comments in her books on the great tits' careful scrutiny of her face and expression, and a very slight indication of expectancy or pleasure might have told 'Star' that she was approaching or had reached the right number of taps with her beak. But this explanation could hardly cover all the incidents described.

Although birds of many different groups have solved problems under experimental conditions, certain species of the tit and crow families seem to be outstanding in their adaptability and quickness in learning from experience. Possibly a varied and unspecialised diet, and the use of feet for holding food, may be factors that favour the development of the curiosity and experimentation that are characteristic of these genera and lead to individual originality in behaviour.

10 *Pests or Pest-controllers?*

———————◆———————

Tits have always been regarded as pests by fruit-growers because of alleged damage to buds in spring and to fruit in autumn, and they have been treated as such. Yarrell recorded in 1837 that a price was paid by churchwardens for the heads of blue tits and their congeners 'under the general name of Tom-tits', and that in one parish seventeen dozen tom-tits' heads were collected.[1] Even today tits are regularly, if unobtrusively, destroyed in some commercial orchards.

One result of this persecution was that ornithological writers of the nineteenth century tried to redress the balance of prejudice against these attractive birds by minimising the damage they inflicted and emphasising their economic value as destroyers of insect pests. This propaganda in favour of the tits was employed on a modest scale by the earlier writers, like Macgillivray, who refers to the blue tit as 'conferring important benefits to man' in its search for food and reports the observation of a pair feeding their young 475 times in nearly seventeen hours.[2] But the defence of the tits reached a climax of enthusiasm in Gould's beautifully illustrated classic of 1862–73, where we read: 'but for them [blue tits] and allied species we should be so overrun by insects that the consequences would be frightful to contemplate.... And I cannot but believe that darkness reigned over that parish whose churchwardens' account contained an item for seventeen dozen tom-tits' heads.' The difficulty of balancing the nuisance of damaged fruit against the benefit of insect pests destroyed is reflected in the rather cautious wording of Witherby's *Handbook* on the food of the blue tit:

'The good done by devouring injurious insects outweighs damage except in special cases.'

In the last twenty years the first detailed quantitative studies of the food consumption of birds and the numbers of the prey species have brought about a drastic reappraisal of the economic value of even the most highly praised 'useful' birds, such as owls and kestrels. The generally accepted view now is that it is the relative abundance of the prey that controls the numbers of predators, not the predators that control the prey. It is even claimed that predators are beneficial to the prey species because they eliminate unhealthy individuals and so improve the breeding stock. (This view is not yet widely held among gamekeepers.)

At the beginning of this century ornithologists accepted that there was a small number of economic enemies to man in the bird world, such as crows and woodpigeons, many more allies, including most of the predators and insectivores, and a number of species of neutral value. In the modern view the enemies remain enemies, but the allies have apparently now become neutrals. How do the common tit species stand in the profit-and-loss account, in the light of information now available? The relationship between predator and prey outlined above could be valid in the majority of cases without necessarily being applicable to all. Moreover, the fact that the numbers of a predatory species are controlled by the available supply of its prey does not exclude the possibility that the prey is also being controlled by the predator: indeed it is probable that in some cases the food shortage that causes 'density-dependent' mortality in a bird species is at least partly due to its own predatory activity. The relationship between food supply and populations of tits has been studied in detail by H. N. Kluijver and L. Tinbergen in the Netherlands, and in England by David Lack and his colleagues, especially J. A. Gibb and Monica Betts, and the discussion in the second part of this chapter is largely based on their published work.

THE DAMAGE

Of the three chief accusations made against tits by horticulturalists, the first is that they destroy buds of fruit trees in spring. Many owners of garden fruit trees will have observed for themselves that blue tits, and sometimes great, coal and marsh tits, peck at the buds of apple and pear trees in spring. But it is important to distinguish the entirely harmless, and probably beneficial, picking of aphids and insect eggs off the outside of the bud, which is a regular feeding practice, especially of blue tits, through the winter and spring, from the actual destruction of buds. Sometimes tits will peck at opening blossom to extract insect eggs and larvae and they may cause some damage to the blossom in the process. Parts of the blossom itself are also occasionally eaten. A. J. Harthan watched a pair of marsh tits detaching single flowers of plum blossom and neatly picking out the ovary; but 'a 4% set of plum blossom results in a full crop of fruit, so the damage done by the tits was negligible.'[3]

Sometimes, though, the buds are definitely torn open by tits and some at least of the contents eaten. Apologists for the birds claim that the bud is opened for the sake of insect food within it. Alfred Newton in the fourth edition of Yarrell's *History of British Birds* (1874) wrote: 'Hardly any portion of the bud itself is eaten; the egg or the insect already lodged there is the morsel sought. The bud of course when picked open is in most cases utterly destroyed, but with it is also destroyed the potential destroyer of more buds than anyone can tell.' This view was supported, or copied, by many subsequent writers; but in 1920 T. A. Coward was more sceptical about the virtue of the blue tit in this respect: 'It is fond of young buds of various trees, and though it may pull them to bits in the hope of finding insects, the damaged and undamaged buds examined after a raid show little sign of having been previously infected.'

More recent research has shown that the buds of trees in spring form an important part of the blue tit's diet, and that normally any animal matter taken with the vegetable is accidental. In the course of her analysis of tits' gizzard-contents in the Forest of Dean, Monica Betts found that, in early spring, nearly all the blue tits had been eating oak buds, and in most samples the bud tissue made up more than half the total gizzard contents. Elsewhere, as was shown in Chapter 7, the buds of other trees, including pear and plum, are occasionally eaten, even, it seems, when these contain no form of insect life. However, the amount of damage caused is too small to have any economic significance. Unlike bullfinches, tits do not make a sustained, systematic attack on fruit buds, and it is unlikely that their brief and sporadic visits to orchards would have any appreciable effect on the eventual fruit crop.

The second major criticism of tits is that they peck small holes in apples and pears during the autumn, so exposing the fruit to further damage from birds and wasps. Not even the most ardent champion of the tit family can deny that blue tits, and sometimes great tits, do this. The hole is almost invariably made on the 'shoulder' of the fruit, near the stalk. The tits seem to prefer pears when they are just ripening, or well-coloured dessert apples. Having once punctured the skin, a blue tit may work at the apple or pear with some persistence for two or three minutes and still only leave a small cavity, but this may then be exploited by starlings or other tits and by wasps. E. N. Wright gave the fruit-grower's point of view: 'Almost inevitably the wound becomes infected by brown rot. This may affect adjacent fruit whilst still on the tree or, which is more serious, the damaged fruit may be put into store and be a source of infection there. During the summer of 1957 fruit pecking by birds was particularly severe and in one orchard of Conference pears in Kent, where counts were made, 15% of the fruits had been damaged in this way. Individual trees showing up to 25% damage were recorded and damage in gardens may reach even higher proportions.'[4]

A later study of bird damage to apples and pears gives further statistical evidence on this subject in three normal years, 1961 to 1963 inclusive, from thirteen orchards in Kent, Sussex, Hampshire, Berkshire and Oxfordshire.[5] Although the report covers damage by all species of birds, the fruits attacked by tits can be distinguished by the small hole on the 'shoulder' and these were separately assessed. In 1961, 2·6 per cent of the 17,675 apples examined showed tit-type damage, but only 0·3 per cent of 40,050 apples in 1962. Cox's Orange Pippins and Bowden's Seedlings and Conference pears were the varieties most frequently attacked.

To put the damage to hard fruit into perspective, R. K. Murton quoted figures from East Malling, Kent, for 1965.[6] Out of 8,828 apples harvested, 429 had to be rejected, and only 27 of these because of injury that could be attributed to birds of any species.

It should be mentioned that great tits sometimes take green peas, and occasionally ripe gooseberries, raspberries and blackcurrants, but the losses involved are very small.

All the evidence at present available indicates that in normal years the damage done by tits to fruit is economically negligible and would not justify the expense of trying to destroy the birds, even if it were legally permissible; in invasion years, when losses may become locally appreciable, it is most unlikely that any such attempt would be effective, owing to the large number of birds involved and their tendency to travel over comparatively long distances under pressure of dense population.

The last major criticism of tits is that they kill and eat honey-bees, and instances of this have, indeed, been recorded for over a century. Gould reluctantly admits the crime in some great and blue tits, and Yarrell mentions the habit in the marsh tit. No doubt beekeepers were well aware of it long before that. This does not prove, however, that any noticeable damage is done to a colony of bees, and it is in fact unlikely that in normal circumstances one or two tits would consume enough bees to affect seriously the strength of a healthy hive.

Inquiries from a number of beekeepers from different parts of England show that many, but by no means all, of them have experienced some destruction of bees by tits. Both great and blue tits have been seen to take live bees, both at the entrance to the hive and in flight. Great tits have been seen to tap on the alighting board of the hive with the result that bees came out and were carried off, but one cannot be sure that the tapping was done with the intention of bringing out the bees and was not simply the familiar exploratory pecking used by tits in so many situations. Both species not infrequently take dead bees from the ground near the hive.

Mrs E. Grayer of Kendal, Westmorland, has kindly given me details of a more sustained attack on a hive in her garden a few years ago. A pair of great tits were feeding six young in a nest-box about 15 metres from a hive. 'The adults would fly to the alighting board of the hive, wait for the bees to land and then quickly snap them up. The tit would then fly to a nearby tree against which it would bang the bee. Whether this was just to kill it or remove the sting we never discovered. We must have lost quite a number of worker bees but I doubt if it made much difference to the honey yield.' The nest-box was not occupied in subsequent years and the bee-killing was not repeated.

This kind of attack was familiar to R. O. B. Manley, the author of a well-known beekeeping manual.[7] 'The tits, blue and great, certainly do kill a good many bees in times when their food is scarce; and in summer, when they are feeding their young, these birds will make a regular habit of catching bees for their babies. These little birds, especially the great tit, will catch a good many bees at the hive entrance when they return loaded and drop down heavily in front of the hive to rest a moment, but I don't think they kill enough bees to make any appreciable difference to the colonies.'

The tits generally succeed in killing and eating bees without suffering any ill-effects. A dead bee I found in a nest-box from which young great tits had just flown had had its sting removed together with the dorsal lower half of the abdomen. Tits never appear to show any fear of bees either near a hive or in blossom, where great tits in particular often encounter them when hunting other insects, although great, blue, marsh, and probably other tits sometimes show considerable nervousness when approached by a wasp. Len Howard wrote that only one of her many tame great tits liked to eat wasps. 'The stings of bees and wasps they always extract with much dexterity before eating.' Great tits clearly recognise that bees and wasps require different treatment from stingless insects. However, on one occasion at least a tit's lack of caution or experience in dealing with bees has had fatal results: W. E. Almond found a juvenile great tit lying dead beside a hive in Cornwall with five stings, which had penetrated both feathers and skin, still in position.[8]

THE BENEFITS

The possible economic benefits conferred by tits are much more difficult to assess than the losses they inflict. All species of tits destroy large numbers of insects, whether in the form of egg, larva, pupa or imago, that harm the interests of man, notably weevils, defoliating caterpillars, codling-moth larvae, 'cabbage' butterflies, scale insects and aphids; and to the bird-loving gardener there is something peculiarly satisfying in seeing a party of tits picking aphids off his rose bushes or plum trees, or watching a breeding pair carrying a rapid succession of caterpillars into their nest-hole or box. It is this last aspect of the tits' apparent benefactions that has chiefly impressed many observers. Both Coward and Witherby quote Professor Newstead's estimate that a pair of great tits will destroy 7,000 to 8,000 insects, chiefly caterpillars, while the young are in the nest.

But impressive though this activity certainly is, most recent research suggests that predation by tits on insect pests in the breeding season is not likely to have a significant effect on their numbers, at least in a woodland environment. The brief peak period of caterpillar population in an oak wood roughly coincides with the time when the young tits are in the nest, but even where the provision of nest-boxes has increased the number of breeding tits they do not usually appear seriously to reduce the numbers of their prey. This at least is the conclusion to be drawn from quantitative studies in both deciduous and coniferous woods in England, as will be shown below. However, the more positive results claimed for the nest-box experiments in Germany which are mentioned later in this chapter also deserve consideration.

In her study of the food of tits in the Forest of Dean, Monica Betts[9] estimated from the rate of accumulation of caterpillar faeces on muslin trays placed under the trees the number of defoliating caterpillars per acre, and, from the number of singing males, occupied nest-boxes and average brood size, the number of tits per acre. She calculated that the insects destroyed averaged 1,344 per tit, yet this only represented 1·4 per cent of the available stock of caterpillars in 1950 and 4·8 per cent in 1951.

On the other hand, an experiment carried out in Scotland in 1949 gave a very different impression of the effect of bird predation on defoliating caterpillars.[10] Ten branches of an oak tree were caged with 13mm (½in) wire netting in early April to exclude birds. In June, ten similar but uncaged control branches were found to be supporting 17 defoliating caterpillars, while the enclosed ones produced 63, chiefly larvae of the winter moth and the oak roller moth *Tortrix viridana*. Although there is always the possibility of misleading inaccuracies in a single experiment, this result clearly suggests that the combined predation of insectivorous birds of several species can have a considerable effect on an insect population.

J. Gibb and M. Betts also studied the food supply of nesting tits in the pine plantations of Thetford Chase on the border of Norfolk and Suffolk, and although there were several differences from the conditions in oakwoods, including a much later peak in the caterpillar population, they concluded that the number of larvae eaten represented only about 3 per cent of those present.[11] However, there was one exception to this generalisation: from 1 May to 15 June 1956, coal tits alone ate some 48,000 larvae or pupae of *Evetria* moths per 10 hectares, representing about 20 per cent of the stock.

Experiments in forests in Germany and the Netherlands have shown that populations of tits and other insectivorous birds can be raised to surprisingly high levels by a dense distribution of nest-boxes, and a marked reduction in the numbers of injurious insects has been reported in some of these areas.[12] In the spring of 1905 a plague of defoliating caterpillars in the neighbourhood of Seebach in Thuringia practically stripped the trees of leaves, but the wood where Baron von Berlepsch, the nest-box pioneer, had placed 2,000 boxes 'was untouched. It stood out like a green oasis among the remaining woods.' There was also an impressive record of reduced infestation by the pine looper moth *Bupalus pinarius* in a boxed area near Steckby on the Elbe over a period of over thirty years. At Neustrelitz a box-protected area of 70 acres yielded only 50 caterpillars of this moth per tree compared with 5,000 per tree in adjoining areas. There was also local success in controlling oak roller moth caterpillars in a forest in Westphalia.

In the Netherlands, L. Tinbergen found that in boxed woods tits removed over 20 per cent of the population of certain insect larvae when these were at a moderate level, a smaller proportion when they were at a high level. The tits apparently preferred to vary their diet and so were less effective in dealing with a plague situation.

The conclusions to be drawn from British and continental studies thus appear to be somewhat contradictory, but the reports from Germany refer to predation by all hole-nesting insectivorous birds and not exclusively by tits, and no one would suggest that tits are the only avian agents of control on insect pests. There is certainly evidence that in winter tits may have a much greater effect on the numbers of their prey than they do in the breeding season. Dr Betts estimated that in the winter of 1950–1 tits probably ate 20 per cent of the female winter moths in the study areas of the Forest of Dean oakwoods. Predation was higher in mild weather, when the moths move about, than in frost, which inhibits movement. J. A. Gibb estimated that blue and coal tits ate about 45 per cent of the larvae of the moth *Ernarmonia conicolana* in Thetford Chase each winter.[13] The larvae spend the winter and pupate just under the surface of scales of the Scots pine. In one winter up to 70 per cent of the larvae were destroyed in places. The destruction of this insect has no economic value to the forester, but the high level of predation suggests that control of insect populations by birds is by no means impossible.

Drs Gibb and Betts also undertook a quantitative study of the food consumption and populations of coal tits and goldcrests in Thetford Chase in five successive winters.[14] Their results were based on counts of the birds in a selected area of Scots pine and Corsican pine, the time they spent feeding in the foliage, the kind of food taken, the average weight consumed daily as indicated by a study of captive tits, and the stock of invertebrate food present in the pines. This last difficult and critical measurement was made by treating samples of foliage with ether and chloroform in closed bags and then shaking out and sorting the animal material. The study revealed wide variations in the quantity of invertebrate food from one winter to another, and a close correlation between severe weather and a reduction of the food stock and also a reduction of the coal-tit population. It was estimated that the birds may sometimes consume a quarter, and occasionally perhaps more than half, of the winter stock of invertebrate food. So if, as is probable, some foods are inaccessible or distasteful to the birds, they will consume well over 25 per cent of the stock of preferred foods during the winter.

Although the economic value of tits in forests has not been conclusively proved, the combined effects of weather and the activities of insectivorous birds and predatory invertebrates appear normally to keep injurious insects within tolerable limits, and the winter feeding of tits may play an important part in this control. Bird predation seems to make little impression on an insect population in a plague situation, but it could help to prevent a plague developing. The available evidence certainly justifies a generous provision of nest-boxes, which are essential to maintain an effective breeding population of hole-nesting birds in plantations of conifers or young broad-leaved trees.

These conclusions are not necessarily valid for gardens and orchards. The fact that tits nesting in gardens have greater difficulty than woodland pairs in raising young (p 181) suggests that insect food is scarcer there and so might be more affected by tit predation. But the short time that most species of moth larvae are available prevents insectivorous birds from seriously depleting their numbers, and it is predation upon adult insects, or certain larvae and pupae that are accessible through the winter, that is most likely to be effective. Notable among the latter is the larva of the codling moth *Carpocapsa pomonella* which emerges through the flesh of apples and pears in summer and spends the autumn and winter in crevices on the trunk and branches of the fruit tree or on the ground.

Localised infestations of other pests may be effectively dealt with by tits and other insectivorous birds. For example a single plum tree in my garden which was very heavily infested with aphids in late July 1969 was searched almost continuously every day for three weeks by blue, coal or marsh tits and willow warblers, and at the end of this period there was hardly an aphis to be found. The birds seemed to form the habit of feeding in this particular tree and continued to search it even when the food supply was practically exhausted.

In an experiment made in Berkshire, the aphids on six shoots of a caged, bird-proof broom bush *Sarothamnus scoparius* declined from 530 to 234 between 6 and 26 June, while on an uncaged bush they declined from 554 to 11.[15] This striking difference was attributed to the activity of birds, chiefly blue tits.

To present a balanced account, one should record that tits, especially great and coal, take considerable numbers of spiders, which may themselves prey upon injurious insects. It is also likely that among the caterpillars taken to the nestlings will be some, perhaps many, carrying eggs, larvae or pupae of parasitic wasps, so that insects generally beneficial to man are being destroyed. These complications illustrate the difficulty of reaching any definite conclusions about the usefulness of insectivorous birds even by the most painstaking calculations of their food intake and the available stock of insect prey.

Perhaps the best method of evaluating the effect of birds on horticulture would be by practical experiment. If a number of cropping hard-fruit trees were enclosed in bird-proof wire netting, with a similar number of control trees outside the enclosure fitted with nest-boxes, both groups being left untreated with insecticide, the comparative quantity and quality of fruit crops over a period of years should give a fair indication of the effectiveness of birds as pest-controllers. A third group of trees, both enclosed and sprayed with insecticide, would provide a comparison between biological and chemical methods. In view of the growing opposition, by beekeepers as well as conservationists, to the use of certain chemical sprays, commercial fruit-growers may wish to consider the possible value of birds as a means of pest control.

11 Domestic Nuisances

PAPER-TEARING

From time to time blue tits, and occasionally great tits, seem to become possessed by a spirit of destructive devilry around houses: they peck putty from window frames, tear garments on washing-lines and come inside to strip paper off walls and attack books and magazines. Fortunately this extraordinary behaviour is strictly seasonal and only occurs on a serious scale once or twice in a decade.

Although the modern practice of garden feeding has been blamed for the boldness and destructiveness of tits at these times, there is, in fact, nothing new in their entering buildings. Indeed, Gilbert White called the blue tit 'a great frequenter of houses' in 1789 in *The Natural History of Selborne*.

In more recent times attention was drawn to the paper-tearing habit by an exceptional outbreak in the autumn of 1949. Lt-Col W. M. Logan-Home organised an inquiry on the subject for the British Trust for Ornithology, and received 242 completed questionnaire forms from Trust members and over 2,000 communications from the general public.[1] Of the Trust questionnaires, 175 recorded paper-tearing by blue tits only, 23 by blue and great tits, 17 by great tits only, with one record each for coal and marsh tits. Most of the great tit records referred to paper-tearing out of doors, but blue tits often invaded houses and many observers described 'blue tits which had been ejected from rooms persistently fluttering and pecking at the windows in their efforts to return'.

Some form of paper was by far the commonest object of the tits' attention. An analysis showed 1,564 attacks on wallpaper, 199 on newspapers and magazines, 114 on covers of books, 110 on name cards on doors, 106 on lampshades, 36 each on letters and passepartout pictures, 34 on cardboard boxes and smaller numbers on other card or paper articles. Wallpaper was usually torn off near the top of a wall with a sideways movement of the tit's head and the strips of paper were dropped immediately without inspection. Various other articles or materials were occasionally affected: 54 instances of attacks on washing on the line were reported, from three to nine incidents involving curtains, leather, stuffing of cushions, chairs, soap, radio aerials and asbestos, and one or two cases of attacks on a wide variety of other objects. At Haileybury College, Hertford, 'a number of tits entered through holes in the dome [of the chapel] and made forty holes through the stucco and asbestos, littering the floor with debris.'

Several observers noted that tits entered south and east windows in the morning and west windows in the afternoon: this was confirmed by Col Logan-Home's experience and agrees with my own. Presumably the interior of the rooms is more clearly visible from outside when they are facing the strongest light.

Fig 5, reproduced from Col Logan-Home's report, shows the strictly seasonal nature of the paper-tearing outbreak in 1949. In other years, too, it has been almost entirely an autumn phenomenon. The major outbreaks have coincided with a high level of tit population, with occasional destructive attacks in houses every year.

A serious incidence of paper-tearing occurred in the autumn of 1957 during the large-scale irruption of tits from northern Europe—fully reported by Cramp, Pettet and Sharrock.[2] As in 1949 the chief culprit was the blue tit: 79 blue tit attacks were recorded, compared with 21 by great tits and 2 by coal tits. Wallpaper was the favourite target (66 instances), followed by books (27), boxes (20), newspapers (17), lampshades (13), notices (9), labels (7) and miscellaneous articles, including plaster, shaving cream, candles and various items of food. 'In one case the extent of the damage led to all the windows being kept firmly closed, but the blue tits still managed to enter through the tiny gap left by the side of the morning paper pushed into the letter-box. In a distributor's food store in Hampshire considerable damage was done

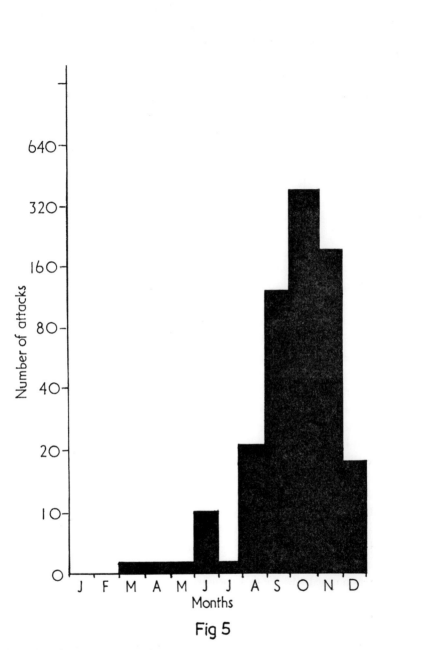

Fig 5

to packaged goods by large flocks of blue tits pecking at the labels and boxes.'

Out of doors, the favourite item was putty: 43 attacks were reported, involving 24 blue tits, 11 great tits, 3 coal tits and 1 marsh tit. (Putty apparently contains a considerable proportion of fish oil and has now become at least an occasional food for tits and other birds. Pepper or paraffin mixed with fresh putty is a recommended deterrent.)

There has been no national inquiry into destructive practices by tits since 1957, and the range and frequency of such incidents in subsequent years is uncertain. They were numerous in north-west England in the autumns of 1970 and 1971 but scarce in 1972 and 1973. In 1971 attacks on paper, clothes and putty were frequent by mid-October, especially in a period of dry, anti-cyclonic weather. On 14 October a blue and a great tit were twice seen eating vermilion paint from an oil painting left out in a garden in north Lancashire.[3]

As the major outbreaks of paper-tearing and house-entering have occurred in years when the blue tit population in late summer has apparently been unusually high, some authorities accept them as simply a reaction to shortage of food.[4] But 80 per cent of the Trust observers recording paper-tearing said that they habitually fed birds. Some reported blue tits tearing up paper wrapped round apples and pears without touching the fruit, and many said that the tits tore up paper and ignored food placed nearby. Col Logan-Home himself kept two well-stocked bird-tables outside his house and on many occasions colour-ringed tits were seen to enter the house and start tearing paper immediately after a good meal. In 1970 and 1971 blue tits in Westmorland frequently left peanuts to begin pecking at window panes and old painted putty round them, and some entered houses. Three juveniles caught inside my house in November 1971 weighed between 11 and 12 grams, well up to the average; and the local beech-mast crop was unusually heavy that autumn.

Another curious fact is that paper-tearing and house-breaking often stop abruptly with an onset of wet or cold weather. Many observers remarked upon this in 1949 and 1957, and it was also noticeable in 1970 and 1971. The activity seems to be greatest on mild, and especially sunny, days and least on cold or rainy ones.

On the basis of the evidence given by W. M. Logan-Home of tits tearing paper when apparently not hungry, R. A. Hinde offered 'A possible explanation of paper-tearing behaviour in birds.'[5] He made a distinction between the hunting and the eating behaviour of tits, as Lorenz had previously done for the predatory birds, and showed that tits often continue searching for food, and sometimes hiding it, when they are not hungry. He also pointed out the similarity between the action of tearing paper and that of tearing dead bark and referred to the fact that blue tits search the dead parts of trees more frequently in autumn than at other times of year. Paper-tearing would thus be an expression of the hunting or food-searching drive. This theory has been taken a stage further by the suggestion that the provision of easy meals on bird-tables and in nut-baskets enables tits to satisfy their physical hunger long before the urge to hunt is exhausted, with the result that the searching drive finds release in destructive activities. The substitution of unshelled peanuts for shelled ones might offer the tits an outlet for their need for pecking and tearing action.

Professor Hinde's hypothesis would explain the frequency of incidents in the vicinity of well-supplied bird-tables, and it also seems compatible with the description given by Miss Len Howard of the behaviour of the tits with which she so generously shared her house. They were certainly not short of food, but attacks on paper, books, stuffed toys, etc, by great tits were frequent and mainly confined to the autumn. Miss Howard refers to these attacks as 'games' or 'pastimes' and remarks that 'Birds, like humans, need occupation as an outlet for their vitality.' A contributor to the 1957 inquiry, Miss M. R. Robinson, had also had blue tits entering her house regularly for some years and found that paper-tearing occurred every year between the end of the moult and the first onset of cold weather, and she believed that it stopped because the tits were too busy searching for food to have time for 'games'. She found that only a small proportion of her blue tits tore paper and surmised that paper-tearing was an intensified form of play indulged in by a few 'rogue' individuals.

My own observations suggest that most of the rogues may be juvenile delinquents. Four blue tits caught inside the house in October–November 1971 were all first-winter birds. All those seen pecking at putty or fluttering at window panes were unringed and none of the twelve colour-ringed adults regularly frequenting the garden was involved.

However, R. A. Hinde's theory offers no explanation of the fact that in fully wild birds paper-tearing is so widespread in some years and restricted in others. Nor does it account for the almost obsessive urge shown by some blue tits in trying to enter houses when there must be abundant bark and other tearable materials outside. The persistent siege of houses is actually one of the most striking features of these periodic outbreaks of paper-tearing.

One of the various theories proposed to explain this strange behaviour is that although the birds may have had enough food there might be some vital constituent lacking, and the raiders were looking for the missing item, possibly some form of animal matter. But there is no direct evidence of any such lack, and it is unlikely that the vital ingredient would need to be urgently sought in paper and inside houses in a fine, warm autumn and not in the cold weather of the following winter. A somewhat imaginative alternative hypothesis propounded some years ago was that the tits became intoxicated by feeding on over-ripe elderberries in a dry autumn and the ensuing damage was done by drunk and disorderly individuals.

The facts that paper-tearing is done by apparently well-fed wild tits, and extensively by house-tamed ones, and that the activity virtually ceases with the onset of winter frosts all support R. A. Hinde's hypothesis; namely that the destructive acts are an expression of the birds' drive to hunt after hunger has been satisfied. The correlation of paper-tearing outbreaks with apparently high tit populations and with new attacks on milk bottles and putty seems to point to food shortage as the cause of the abnormal behaviour of tits in certain years; but this behaviour could be a direct reaction to high numbers rather than to any resulting hunger. The well-known effects of overcrowding upon lemmings, rats and humans may not be strictly comparable, but a mild avian counterpart is a possibility. In autumns when the blue tit population appears to be exceptionally high the birds give an impression of restless excitability. Investigating and pecking at a wide variety of objects is a regular feature of this excessive activity and could easily lead to the discovery of the edibility of soft putty and the contents of milk bottles.

The efforts to enter houses may result from the urge shown by many birds and mammals, especially when young, to explore their environment. Exploration is of great value to a bird in providing it with a detailed knowledge of food sources, roosting places, dangers and refuges within its normal range. W. H. Thorpe writes that juvenile great tits are 'at their maximum of exploratory activity at about thirteen weeks'. This would roughly coincide with an autumnal season of house-entering. It is also in the autumn, when juveniles and displaced adults are establishing themselves in a certain area for the winter, that a thorough reconnaissance is of special value.

Although it is still not possible to offer a confident and comprehensive explanation of the destructive and invasive activities of blue and great tits it seems likely that one or more of the factors mentioned above—an unsatisfied urge to hunt, a reaction to large numbers and the need to explore—are involved in most instances.

MILK BOTTLES

The actions of experienced great or blue tits on the metal-foil cap of a milk bottle are brisk and business-like. One or two sharp blows puncture the foil, which is then torn off in strips and dropped. A large hole is quickly opened, and sometimes the whole cap is removed. The tits then drink the creamy top of the milk. Although the actions are very similar to those of paper-tearing, and although the paper-tearing epidemics coincide on occasions with a new peak in attacks on milk bottles, bottle-opening is, obviously, a highly rewarding activity for the birds concerned, while paper-tearing produces no edible benefits.

Bottle-opening is a much more recent development than paper-tearing, no doubt simply because the use of milk bottles with cardboard or metal-foil caps which a bird can puncture or remove is a comparatively new feature of the western-European way of life. Even now this habit is not by any means universal and may only be a temporary phase, as the use of hard metal caps or of plastic or waxed containers tends to increase.

However, the first use of bottles with card or foil caps for milk delivery made it possible to trace the origin and spread of a new feeding habit in a group of bird species in unusual, though necessarily still incomplete, detail. A short history of the opening of milk bottles by birds in the British Isles was compiled by James Fisher and R. A. Hinde.[6] It was based on an inquiry organised by the British Trust for Ornithology and on information received through newspaper correspondence and from other sources. A supplement gave some information about the development of the habit in other parts of north-west Europe and outlined a theory of the processes involved in learning to open a milk bottle.[7]

The credit for the first discovery and exploitation of this valuable new food source should go to an unspecified tit at Swaythling near Southampton which opened the first bottle in the British Isles some time in 1921. (It is possible that this achievement was anticipated by two years in Denmark.) Milk bottles at that time were sealed with waxed cardboard, and tits developed various techniques for dealing with this. If the card was not pressed right in, a tit might lever it off by inserting its bill under a crease in the cardboard, or a hole might be pecked right through the middle, or the card torn off in strips. When metal-foil caps were introduced, the birds coped with the new problem without difficulty. By the end of 1947, 400 identifications had been made of tits opening bottles: of these 246 were blue tits, 142 great tits, 11 coal tits and 1 marsh tit. There were also reports of other species opening bottles, the most frequent being house sparrows (19 records), starlings (13) and blackbirds (12).

In a series of six maps, Fisher and Hinde showed how the bottle-opening habit had developed in the British Isles between 1921 and 1947. These maps show a clustering of later records round a comparatively small number of isolated new occurrences and give the impression that 'this source of food was actually discovered *de novo* by only a small proportion of the tit population and was then passed on in some way to other individuals'. In a recent letter, however, Professor Hinde stressed that 'the geographic spread was most probably due to the spread of milk bottles, "imitation" operating only at the local level'.

The lack of records from large areas in Scotland and Ireland could be explained simply by the absence of milk bottles, but there were also large centres of population in England where no bottle-opening had been recorded up to 1947, and even where the habit was wide-spread there were often blank pockets, as is still true today.

The large-scale irruption of tits into the British Isles in the autumn of 1957 was accompanied by a new outburst of bottle-opening, and the report by Cramp, Pettet and Sharrock recorded 49 instances of it in new localities that autumn. However, the map of reported incidents does not differ greatly from Fisher and Hinde's map for 1947, and the proportion of tit species involved was similar. A new feature was the definite late-autumn peak in bottle-opening, coinciding with a similar rise and fall in attacks on paper and putty. In normal years most attacks on milk bottles are reported in winter, perhaps because this is when most tits are found near houses.

Since 1957 there has been no national inquiry into bottle-opening by birds—but it is of interest that blue tits in the Isle of Man first opened bottles at Onchan on the east coast in the mid-1950s, and not till about 1970 ten miles away north of Snaefell.[8] However, the habit must now be endemic in Britain and will not die out as long as foil-capped bottles are in use. Nevertheless, many great and blue tits apparently do not recognise milk bottles as a source of food, others only investigate a bottle that has already been opened, and only a few actually tear open the metal caps. The expert birds, however, im-mediately recognise and attack exposed bottles even if they have been given no opportunity of doing so for four or five months. In my own garden between 27 December 1970 and 5 March 1971 7 different colour-ringed blue tits and two great tits (the resident pair) were seen to open milk bottles, a further 6 blue tits enlarged a hole already begun but never started one, and ten others drank from opened bottles without attacking the foil cap. Visiting coal and marsh tits showed no interest in the milk bottles whether capped or open.

There is nothing new or unexpected in the tits' method of opening milk bottles. The puncturing action is that normally used in opening nuts and seeds, and the tearing movement is the regular method of removing dead bark from branches to discover insects under it. It is not so obvious how the pioneer tits first discovered that the bottles contained food and how the knowledge of this fact and of the vul-nerability of the caps is passed on to other individuals.

Exploratory pecking is a characteristic tit habit, whether the bird is actually searching for food or finding an outlet for its superfluous 'hunting drive'. When milk bottles were sealed with waxed cardboard, this material would naturally attract the attention of tits in a 'paper-tearing autumn', and the hollow sound produced by tapping on either a cardboard or a foil bottle cap might act as a stimulus to further exploration. So the discovery that the contents of milk bottles are edible could well be made accidentally by garden-haunting tits in the course of their pecking and testing activity. After this discovery the opening process becomes purposive and not just exploratory: this is very obvious from the confident vigour with which the experts attack a foil cap.

When tits see others of their kind feeding, they are often drawn to investigate the food source, and this would lead other tits to opened bottles. Whether they actually learn the technique of bottle-opening by imitation from experienced birds is debatable, but such an ability would help to explain the very rapid spread of the habit in the high population autumns when gangs of milk thieves follow the delivery vans. At these times, their determination is especially remarkable; tits may be observed removing cloths, tin lids and even stones placed on bottle tops to protect them.

The exploitation of this new food supply seems in many ways so purposeful and effective that the apparently 'unintelligent' nature of some of the birds' reactions is a surprise. For example, on three days in late December I put out, side by side, a full milk bottle and an empty one, closed with similar foil caps, and noted the pecking attacks made on them. Out of 41 attacks, 16 were made on the empty bottle. The empty bottle was attacked by nine different blue tits and two different great tits, and its cap torn open as effectively as that of the full bottle. Possibly only the cap, and perhaps also the neck, of the bottle is associated with food by the tits. I have only very occasionally seen a blue tit take a tentative peck at the glass of a milk bottle, full or empty, but when a glass jar of peanuts with a metal foil cap was put out with the milk bottles both blue and great tits pecked persistently at the glass for three days and only an occasional bird tapped briefly at the foil cap. When the metal foil cap was replaced by a thin transparent cover of cellophane this was torn open on the second day and then some tits picked nuts out from the top, but others still continued to peck at the glass jar. It appeared that the peanuts were recognised as food, eliciting a direct approach, while milk was not.

Several observers have reported that tits prefer bottles with the gilt caps that are used for the rich creamy milk of Channel Island cattle, and in 1957 in three cases the birds were said to have detected the deception when the caps of the bottle were exchanged: they continued to go for the Jersey milk even without the gilt cap. In my own experience both great and blue tits tend to attack a gilt-capped bottle before a red-capped one when offered the choice, but the preference is not invariable, and the same individual will often try both colours in turn. In view of tits' rather limited discrimination in the sense of taste (see Chapter 12), any difference in response might be attributable to their preference for certain colours rather than for special types of milk.

12 *Welcome Guests*

GARDEN FEEDING

Two hundred years ago Gilbert White of Selborne watched with 'delight and admiration' as great tits, hanging with back downwards, drew straws lengthwise from the eaves of houses so as to extract the flies between them, 'in such numbers that they quite defaced the thatch and gave it a ragged appearance'. His delight and admiration were probably not shared by the occupants of the houses; his blend of scientific curiosity and aesthetic pleasure in watching birds was exceptional at that time. However, as early as 1825 J. F. M. Dovaston, a Shropshire landowner, wrote to Bewick describing his 'Ornithotrophe', a wooden trencher suspended from a cord stretched between two trees outside his study window. 'This I trim with food and with a wand from within can slide it to and fro along the line . . . I have also perches about and near it and fasten half-picked bones and flaps of mutton to the trees.' This novelty was publicised by Bewick and copied by 'many gentle-minded people'. But it was not until the severe winter of 1890–1, when all the leading newspapers advocated feeding birds, that it became generally popular in Britain.[1]

The bird-feeding habit has grown rapidly, with only temporary setbacks in the two world wars resulting from the shortage of edible fats. But it is in the last twenty years that the cult of tit-feeding has developed most rapidly, as shown by the tremendous increase in the range of nest-boxes, bird-tables, tit-feeders and tit foods (and a bird-bath 'shallow enough for a blue tit') offered by commercial firms.

It could be argued that the householder with a well-stocked bird-table or nut-basket is doing a disservice to the forester and fruit-grower by withdrawing tits from their beneficial winter predation on insects in woods and orchards. Blue tits in particular are attracted into towns, villages and rural gardens from their natural woodland habitat in considerable numbers by the availability of an abundant food supply, but most of them probably continue to take some insect food, and the garden largesse may be helping to maintain a higher tit population through the year.

All the British tits will come to suitable food put out near houses, but the numbers and the species will depend upon the geographical location and the surrounding habitats. A town or suburban bird-table will nearly always attract some blue and great tits and often one or two coal tits, but it may be a very leisurely visitation compared with the hive-like activity at some rural feeding-stations. In a district rich in broad-leaved woodland, twenty or more blue tits with great, coal and (in England and Wales) occasional marsh tits may be watched together in a bewildering succession of hurried feeds, threat displays, 'supplanting attacks' and pursuits. Willow tits, even where comparatively abundant, often ignore bird-tables, perhaps because of a preference for an insect diet. They are not particularly shy and at some feeding-stations are the most approachable of the tit visitors. Long-tailed tits do not often become regular attenders, but short occasional visits from parties of them are not uncommon in rural areas, and for a few minutes the garden seems alive with tiny bodies, delicately balanced tails and 'tupping' and trilling calls.

In a pilot study for a Garden Birds Feeding Survey conducted by the British Trust for Ornithology in the winter of 1970–1, blue tits were recorded at 97 per cent of the sample 152 feeding-stations, great tits at 89 per cent, coal tits at 53 per cent, marsh tits at 17 per cent, long-tailed tits at 13 per cent and willow tits at 10 per cent.

In the neighbourhood of coniferous forest the proportions may be quite different. In parts of the Spey valley near the old Caledonian Forest a constant stream of coal tits pours into any garden feeding-station, while blue and great tits are scarce and marsh and willow tits unknown. Not infrequently a crested tit will arrive, dominant and aggressive, announcing its presence with the call expressively described by a crofter as 'gurrning', and keeping the coal tits at bay.

All these tits are acrobatic and adaptable in extracting food from a wide variety of nutshells, bags, wire baskets and other containers. They can feed efficiently clinging to the side of a nut-basket or hanging upside down from its base. Great tits adopt the latter position rather less often than the smaller species, but the belief that they are anatomically incapable of hammering and tearing effectively while hanging upside down seems untenable. If peanuts in a container are only accessible from below, great tits will peck at them vigorously for more than a minute at a time in this position, and I have watched one with a crippled leg feed quite successfully while hanging from one foot. On the other hand, great tits do seem to have greater difficulty than the smaller species in alighting in an upside-down position, and occasionally they miss their grip when attempting to do so. I have never seen this happen with the other tits. It is said that a house-fly alights on a ceiling by executing a half-roll sideways: a tit normally achieves a similar position by performing a half-loop, throwing the head back and the legs and body forward and upward, so that it ends up facing in the direction from which it arrived.

A garden feeding-station offers an attractive food supply in an abnormally restricted area, so that the kind of competition that is only occasionally found in nature is maintained in an intensified form over a long period. This situation offers exceptional opportunities for observing the relationships between the different species of tits. In general, as one would expect, the smaller species are submissive to the larger. Thus great tits usually dominate all the other species, blue tits dominate all but great tits, and coal tits are inferior to the others, including marsh, willow and crested. However, it is not at all unusual for individual blue tits, especially the male in whose territory the feeding-station is situated, to dominate all others, including great tits and even greenfinches and house-sparrows. Blue tits are, in fact, exceptionally courageous and aggressive birds for their size. I have seen crested tits driven off by great tits but have not observed a confrontation between blue and crested tits: an encounter between males of these species, each in his own territory, would be interesting to watch; I would estimate the odds as slightly in favour of the blue tit. Willow tits dominate coal tits at a feeding-station but are very reluctant to approach a food supply held by great or blue tits. Long-tailed tits generally seem to give way to the *Parus* species.

The superiority of the dominant species is shown in various ways. For example, if a great or blue tit is in occupation of a nut-bag, a marsh or coal tit will generally wait for it to leave. A marsh or coal tit feeding when a great or blue tit arrives usually flies away or is driven off by a 'supplanting attack' or some form of threat display. In a supplanting attack the aggressor normally arrives from above and behind a feeding bird as though about to alight on its back: the victim nearly always gives way before actual contact is made. 'Threat display' is a general expression used to cover various postures and movements by which one bird shows some degree of hostility towards another. Ethologists believe that these postures are a result of the simultaneous elicitation of behaviour patterns of attack and fleeing.

A. W. Stokes analysed the separate elements of displays by blue tits at a feeding-station, and then tried to predict the outcome of an encounter between two individuals from the combinations of these elements they used.[2] He found that when a blue tit raised its crest (Plate, p 34) and fluffed its body feathers it never attacked and in 90 per cent of instances it escaped, but for other elements of display the probability of correct forecast was 52 per cent or less. He concluded that 'what a bird actually does following a specific posture appears to depend upon a combination of internal and external stimuli which are only partly reflected in the bird's postures'. This implies that the postures do not give fully reliable signs of a bird's intentions to its opponent, and this uncertainty may lead to actual conflict.

Nevertheless, a great tit in full aggressive display, when in possession of a food supply, is a formidable sight (Plate, p 120). It takes up a crouching position with wings raised and spread and tail expanded and depressed and the feathers of the nape ruffled; the feathers of the crown are flattened and the bill is pointed either downwards or straight at the adversary. The mandibles may be parted, but this seems to indicate an intention to stay rather than attack. (In an occasional spectacular variation, a great tit may hang upside down from a perch with outspread wings and tail like a displaying bird of paradise.) Less intense forms of the 'horizontal display' are often seen, and separate components of it may be used independently. This type of display is regularly used towards other great tits as well as birds of different species at feeding places. The 'vertical display' described in Chapter 3 is the normal form in territorial disputes, but it is comparatively rare at a feeding-station until reproductive rivalry develops in February and March.

The 'horizontal display' and its various elements are frequently used by blue tits as well as by great tits. Occasionally, coal and marsh tits are seen to use at least some of these postures, but these species usually do little more than flatten their bodies and flick their wings. Their threatening attitudes are normally only momentary and are not as fully developed as those of great and blue tits. When coming for food, a marsh tit will often give vocal expression to its irritation if it is kept waiting, but generally avoids conflict with other species. Coal tits make hurried, nervous visits, sometimes awaiting their turn in an alert posture with raised crown feathers—an indication of anxiety and indecision common to all tit species. It may well be the infrequent use of definite threat postures by coal tits that accounts for the constant attacks and pursuits to be seen when a number of them are competing for food.

Actual physical combat is not uncommon, especially between blue tits. A bird in occupation of a nut-basket will try to push off a new arrival with one foot; if the other bird grips the extended foot both tits may fall off and then either break away or, more rarely, continue the struggle with pecking and biting.

The casual observer usually has little idea of the number of tits visiting his garden. At my own house in south Westmorland in the mild winter of 1970–1, I caught and marked with plastic coloured rings, between 16 November and 28 February inclusive, 162 blue tits, 26 great tits, 12 coal tits and 5 marsh tits. But these numbers are insignificant compared with those recorded at Oxford by C. M. Perrins.[3] On several occasions he caught more than 100 tits at one bird-table in a single morning, and in five visits within a fortnight to a well-provided table he caught over 250 great and blue tits.

The origins and movements of these large numbers of tits have not been fully elucidated. Some of the Oxford birds seemed to travel around in small parties from one bird-table to another. Dr Perrins writes that others 'come from woodland outside the cities; they may fly two or three miles to get food. Some appear to do this daily, "commuting" to the gardens and returning to the woods to roost . . .

Woodland tits do this only when they are short of food.' This explanation is supported by the fact that there is usually a marked increase in tit activity at bird-tables in the latter part of the winter when the supply of natural food would be dwindling. In spells of severe weather earlier in the winter there is also a marked decrease in the number of tits in the woods and a corresponding increase at bird-tables in neighbouring towns and villages.

The constant activity round a peanut container in cold weather may give the impression that several tits are using the same food source almost continuously through the day. However, observation of colour-ringed birds shows that this is not normally the case. The following table of marked birds at my feeding-station in south Westmorland shows the quick succession of different individuals, particularly blue tits, at the food supply, even without allowing for visits by unringed birds.

TABLE II   COLOUR-RINGED TITS SEEN IN 21 WATCHES, 15.12.70 to 24.3.71

	Blue tit	Great tit	Coal tit	Marsh tit
Highest count of different birds in one hour	39	5	5	1
Mean of 20 one-hour watches	28·7	2·1	1·5	0·25
Two-hour watch, 23.12.70	46	4	2	0

Of the colour-ringed blue tits seen at the food, an average of 40 per cent appeared only once in an hour, a further 23 per cent twice and 14 per cent three times. A single bird, the dominant resident male, returned up to eight times in an hour. Observation confirms that the majority of these blue tits were taking a considerable proportion of natural food, and some were also visiting other bird-tables. Five of my ringed birds were seen during the winter at one table 800m away, but none at another closely watched one 450m in another direction. The direct route to the former feeding place would be over houses and gardens, to the latter almost entirely through woodland. It is possible that blue tits actively search the more built-up areas for bird-tables and nut-baskets and travel further in this way than in their woodland hunts for insects. Two first-winter blue tits with numbered metal rings, frequent attenders from early December to mid-March, had been ringed in a rural habitat 5km away in August and September.

Some blue tits are regular visitors at a feeding-place from autumn to spring, some pay only occasional visits and others may come once and not be seen again. A pioneer study of colour-ringed blue tits made in a midland suburb by Hugh Kenrick showed that roughly three-eighths of them were fully resident, nesting in the garden and coming to the table in winter, one-eighth nested in the garden but were not seen in winter, one-quarter were winter visitors, generally from January to March and then not till the following year, and one-quarter were winter passage migrants, occurring mostly in February and March.[4]

In the winter of 1970-1 I recorded the appearance of 162 colour-ringed blue tits at my feeding-station on forty days from mid-December to the end of March during observation periods varying from forty minutes to three hours. The attendance chart presents a complex pattern, but an analysis of the results may be summarised as follows:

1   42 blue tits (28 per cent of those ringed) were sighted in every month after the one in which they were ringed.

2   13 of these were recorded in more than half the watches. The male who occupied the nearest nest-box in 1971 scored 39 attendances out of 40.

3   A further 16 (11 per cent) reappeared in March although not recorded in one or more of the intermediate months.

4   38 (25 per cent) of the blue tits ringed were not seen again after their release.

Thus a minimum of 39 per cent of the birds ringed survived the winter and were still visiting the feeding-station at the end of it. There was no indication of a wave of passage migrants at any particular season, but rather a suggestion of nomadic individuals or parties calling briefly to feed at any time during the winter. For example, on 22 January, 31 out of 77 visits observed in an hour were by unringed birds. Although some tits ringed in the earlier part of the winter reappeared in March there was no increase in the number of unringed birds. On the contrary the proportion of unringed visiting blue tits decreased steadily through the winter: they made up 27 per cent of the total visitors in December, 25 per cent in January, 15 per cent in February, 11 per cent in March.

During the following winter, 1971-2, also a very mild one, 38 of the colour-ringed blue tits returned to the feeding-station. Twenty of them first appeared before 31 December, the other 18 between 1 January and 24 March. This appears to confirm the belief that many blue tits only come to garden food in the latter part of the winter.

Sightings of 26 marked great tits, 12 coal tits and 5 marsh tits suggested that these species are more sedentary than blue tits: casual vagrant visitors are comparatively uncommon.

Miss Howard remarks on the individual food preferences of her house-tamed great tits.[5] One or two of them refused cheese, or certain kinds of cheese, and a few were 'fussy about the type of nut', but she never had a tit that refused peanuts. Although a few observers report a preference for composite foods such as oatmeal set in fat, regular watching confirms the popularity of peanuts but reveals some differences between the species. When offered an unimpeded choice between peanuts, fat, cheese and bread, great, blue, coal and marsh tits all selected peanuts first on more than half their visits, great and marsh tits showing a particularly strong preference for them with 95 per cent and 83 per cent of their first choices. Blue tits were the most varied in their tastes and only they took an appreciable quantity of bread (10 per cent of choices), while coal tits showed a well-marked taste for fat (39 per cent of choices; blue tits were next with 12 per cent).

This discrimination in the choice of food raises the question of how birds in general, and tits in particular, recognise the edibility or inedibility of various objects and how they develop a preference for one kind of food over another. It is not obvious which senses are involved in making these distinctions, but for tits the first stimulus to test the edibility of an object is probably a visual one. Colour, shape, size and, in the case of living prey, movement, could all play a part in stimulating investigation.

In the course of three winters, 1969–71, a series of tests with coloured food items revealed some fairly consistent trends. At intervals of some months garden-feeding great and blue tits were offered a choice of equal quantities of small cubes of nut or pieces of shredded suet stained red, green and violet with vegetable dyes or left in natural colour (white). In five tests the white food was always finished first, and red was second in four of them. Green was taken last in four tests, violet in one.

The first choices of blue and great tits while all colours were still available were: blue tit: 34 white, 6 red, 2 green; great tit: 25 white, 1 red, 1 violet. A hand-tamed blue tit when offered the full choice picked white seven times out of nine, green twice. Without white, he chose red seven times, green six, violet once.

The preference for white foods is not surprising, as so many seeds and eggs and larvae of insects are pale in colour, and so are most of the offerings on bird-tables. The reasons for the order of preference of the other colours are not obvious.

Shape and size are apparently of little significance in the recognition of 'garden' foods. When offered a choice of bleached almonds in their natural shape or cut into squares, rectangles, triangles, circles, rings or small fragments, tits of the four common species made a random selection. Apparently any whitish object put out close to a regular feeding-place is tested for edibility, irrespective of its shape.

Most birds are thought to possess only a rudimentary sense of smell, but it has been suggested that blue and great tits might use smell to solve certain rudimentary 'intelligence tests', and it has been further claimed that blue tits could be trained to respond to odours as signals.[6] W. B. Yapp states that 'although always small compared with those of most mammals the olfactory lobes of birds do in fact show a considerable range of size', and there are other physiological indications that 'while smell would appear to be an unimportant sense it seems unlikely that it is completely lacking.'[7] But I have found no evidence that tits are either attracted to food by its smell or repelled by an unfamiliar scent on a normal foodstuff. Pieces of fresh and toasted cheese, a familiar food to the tested birds, concealed under a single thickness of loose cloth on a bird-table were never discovered or apparently noticed by any of the blue, great or coal tits frequenting the table. Pieces of nut and cheese soaked in garlic essence, commercial paraffin, lavender water and vinegar were all taken without hesitation by blue and great tits, which showed no preference for the untreated samples also available. Strongly scented toilet soap was also readily taken, although, as is shown below, some birds rejected abnormal foods after eating a few morsels.

Of the closely related sense of taste in birds, C. J. Duncan wrote: 'The striking feature is the small number of buds: in the domestic pigeon a maximum of 59 and an average of 37.'[8] For comparison, a man has an average of about 9,000 taste buds, a rabbit about 17,000. The results of a series of simple experiments with unnaturally flavoured foods can be summarised as follows:

1   **Nut soaked in brine.** One blue tit took 7 or 8 pecks; another flew off after nibbling the second mouthful in its bill. A marsh tit fed briefly. After four days more of the salted nut had been eaten than of the untreated 'control' nut.

2   **Nuts and cheese soaked in commercial paraffin.** Ten different blue tits fed, one taking 25 pecks and another returning twice; two great tits fed; one coal tit fed steadily for about 20 seconds, another shook fragments from its bill after five pecks and flew off; one marsh tit took four pecks, wiped its bill several times and flew off.

3   **Cheese soaked in vinegar.** Three blue tits and two great tits fed normally, one great tit eating steadily for about 30 seconds.

4   **Brazil nuts steeped in bitter aloes.** Some blue tits took up to 12 pecks and one returned for more, others wiped their bills after two or three pecks and flew off. A great tit took nine pecks, and a coal tit only one. After one day the nuts were left untouched by all visiting tits.

5   **Scented toilet soap.** Six different blue tits took one to five pecks each; one great tit two pecks. None returned for more and the soap was ignored on subsequent days.

It will be seen that the only offering immediately and unanimously rejected was the soap, and even so it took two blue tits five bites to discover its inedibility. Bitter aloes flavouring also proved unacceptable but took longer to detect. Coal and marsh tits seemed generally more sensitive to taste than blue or great tits. Some individual tits showed distaste for brine and paraffin, others seemed unaffected. This does not, of course, prove that the birds were unable to detect the abnormality, but the acceptance of the unnatural and pervasive paraffin suggests that taste in itself is probably not a major factor in the choice of foods by most tits. As untreated foods were available during these tests the birds were not compelled by hunger to take unpalatable matter. However, captive great tits have been found to show a preference for glucose solution over plain water, and some distaste for sour, salt and bitter solutions.[9]

It would appear that tits are first attracted to a possible food, at least at or near a feeding-station, by its colour and not by its shape or smell, and the final decision on edibility probably depends on a combination of taste and the feel of the substance in the bird's mouth and gullet.

GARDEN NEST-BOXES

Charles Waterton, the Yorkshire naturalist who died in 1865, is generally regarded as the pioneer of artificial nest-sites for conservation purposes, although nesting tits were occasionally assisted even before his time. Alfred Newton relates how an earthenware bottle left to drain in a tree on a Northumberland farm was occupied annually by blue tits from 1779 or 1785 at least until 1873, except for one year when the farmer omitted to remove the old nest and another when great tits usurped the site.[10] With selective benevolence the farmer shot the great tits so as to maintain the blue tits' occupation.

The wooden nest-box for tits was promoted in Britain towards the end of the nineteenth century by the Royal Society for the Protection of Birds, while in Germany Baron von Berlepsch and others were putting up thousands of boxes in forests. Great care was taken to give these boxes a natural appearance by using hollowed-out sections of log, but experience soon showed that great and blue tits and pied fly-catchers were just as likely to nest in a plain wooden box as in one bored out of a log or disguised with strips of bark. One is reminded of Richard Kearton's early efforts at bird photography, when he used an elaborately constructed artificial cow as a hide, only to discover later that a simple tent was just as effective.

Tits will readily accept boxes made of metal, plastic, sawdust compound or concrete. At least these are all waterproof and are immune to the onslaughts of great spotted woodpeckers, which can cause serious trouble with wooden boxes, but concrete lids are easily broken and metal, plastic and concrete boxes may become painfully hot for nestling tits if not carefully sited. And although the feathered tenant apparently has no objection to these substitutes for timber, some humans will find them lacking in aesthetic appeal.

The box should have a large enough floor area for a brood of young to overflow from the nest in the later stages of growth, and should be deep enough to discourage premature flight by the nestlings and to frustrate the extended paw of marauding cat or squirrel. Perches on or close to the box should be avoided; they are not needed by the tits and may help predators to reach the entrance hole. A hinged or removable lid or front or side panel is desirable, so that the contents of the box can be examined and old nests removed, but the lid should be latched or fixed in some way to prevent opening by cats or squirrels. The lid should project over the entrance hole to keep out rain and the whole box should be completely weatherproof.

The wetting of the nest and consequent chilling of eggs or nestlings is one of the commonest causes of failure by tits to rear broods in nest-boxes. If the box is placed on a tree, care should be taken to see that rain water does not run down the trunk and soak into the back of the box. It should also be shaded from the heat of the midday sun and yet have a fairly open approach for the parent birds. For security from predatory mammals and interfering humans, nest-boxes should be 3 or 4 metres (10–12ft) above the ground. Cleaning out the boxes at the end of the breeding season helps to prevent infestation by parasites.

There is no doubt that nest-boxes do attract tits to breed in gardens: the small round hole seems to invite the attention of both great and blue tits, especially the former. Unfortunately there are several indications that gardens, or at all events small ones in towns or housing estates, are not usually a favourable breeding habitat for the birds. The clutches laid by both blue and great tits in gardens are, on average, smaller than those of the same species in woodland, and it has been shown that clutch size is adapted to the food potential of the habitat (see Chapter 4). C. M. Perrins found that blue tits had an average clutch of 11 eggs in woodland near Oxford but only about 9 in gardens in the city; the corresponding averages for great tits were nearly 9 and 7½ respectively. Even with these reduced clutches the city birds usually lost between a third and a half of their young before fledging and the rest left the nest in very poor condition. It was not unusual for both great and blue tits to lose the whole brood before fledging.

The nestlings require a diet rich in protein, and in broad-leaved woodland this is abundantly supplied by small caterpillars, which are especially numerous on oak leaves. This kind of food is comparatively scarce in a small garden and, although aphids may provide an adequate substitute for caterpillars for the first day or two after the eggs have hatched, the parent tits could never collect enough, even from the most neglected rose bushes, to satisfy the daily needs of seven or eight half-grown nestlings. Moreover, it is not always true in the tit world that 'mother knows best' about food for her family. I have seen a blue tit carry 38 beakfuls of white bread into a nest-box in quick succession —though in spite of this strange diet the seven young all subsequently flew strongly from the box. Len Howard describes a brood of great tits which was fed largely on mutton fat: the nestlings never developed proper feathers and the three that left the box were unable to fly and were killed by cats within half an hour. A whole brood of well-feathered blue tit nestlings has been found dead after being fed on peanuts, which they were unable to digest.

Bigger gardens, with a few large trees, or town or village gardens near parks or woods, may provide conditions which are little inferior to woodland itself. Blue tits will regularly fly over 180 metres (200 yards) from their garden nest site to the nearest oak tree to collect caterpillars, and even a single large oak left in the middle of a housing estate or on a school playing-field may enable tits within this distance to raise normal broods in small gardens. In a favourable year the extra travelling seems to offer no insuperable difficulty. The perils of cat and car have also been urged as an argument against encouraging urban breeding by tits, but it seems very doubtful whether losses caused by cat predation or road casualties are heavier than those due to sparrow-hawks, woodpeckers, grey squirrels and weasels in the woods.

To sum up, blue and great tits would be unlikely to raise broods successfully in a small garden with no large trees nearby. Where there are well-grown oaks within 250 metres a garden box may be worth trying; but if experience shows that the tits are not rearing more than two-thirds of their brood, it would be kinder to remove the box, or to enlarge the hole to admit fully urbanised house-sparrows and starlings. If conditions prove satisfactory, a garden nest-box placed in view of a convenient window can provide weeks of interesting and entertaining armchair bird-watching.

An 'observation box' with a glass window in the back or side is a valuable aid to studying the details of the behaviour of nestlings and parents inside the box. If this window is closely fitted against a corresponding opening in the wall of a dark shed or hut one can watch every activity at the nest at a range of a few inches without any disturbance of the birds. Further information can be obtained by regular inspection of nest contents, weighing of nestlings, etc; but the garden box-watcher should consider how much disturbance is advisable or justifiable. Great tits vary individually in their tolerance of disturbance, but females may desert the nest if frightened off it at any stage of incubation. Two painstaking Polish zoologists discovered that 'only 20 per cent' of great tits deserted their nests when caught in the box, and that desertions were commonest in the egg-laying period.

Hatching time is another sensitive period. Blue tits are remarkably courageous and persevering in their attachment to eggs and young, but if caught at the nest a parent may occasionally desert even well-feathered nestlings. Although a biologist with a definite programme of inquiry may find it necessary to risk a small percentage of desertions in the course of his study, most amateur bird-watchers would rather remain in ignorance of a few technical details than feel responsible for the abandonment of eggs or nestlings in their own gardens. Trapping and ringing, which is only permissible for qualified ringers, should also be employed only for a definite purpose, and with great care.

13 Life and Death

The life of the average tit is hazardous and short. Each pair of great or blue tits in Britain and northern Europe normally rears between five and ten nestlings a year, and yet, in spite of considerable fluctuations from one year to another, there is no sign of a permanent increase in the tit population. So on average only two out of the whole family, parents and young, survive to breed the following year. Dr D. W. Snow calculated, by a comparison of the numbers of first-year and fully adult specimens in museum collections, that the annual mortality of adult blue tits in Britain was about 70 per cent.[1] This was higher than for any other species whose mortality rate had been calculated. In the Netherlands, H. N. Kluijver estimated the annual death rate for first-year great tits at 86·8 per cent and for older birds at 49 per cent.[2] In Marley Wood the annual mortality ranged from 47–83 per cent (pages 189–90).

Yet there is remarkably little direct evidence of the actual causes of death. One might expect that these intensely active little birds would have such a high metabolic rate as to be physically incapable of surviving more than four or five years, but in fact this is not the case. Since 1960 the annual reports of the Ringing & Migration Committee of the British Trust for Ornithology have given for each listed species the total of ringed birds recovered in the year and the maximum age each attained. Table 12 summarises the data for ten years on maximum ages reached by individual great and blue tits, and by three other species with comparable totals of recoveries.

So blue tits can survive in the wild to the age of 11 years, and at least one individual recovered in each of the ten years was over 7 years old. As longevity is usually roughly proportional to body size, it is interesting that elderly birds occurred most frequently among blue tits, the smallest species of the five in this sample. There are comparatively few recoveries for the other tit species, but the oldest long-tailed tit recovered, out of 70 in six years, had reached the age of $4\frac{1}{12}$ years.

TABLE 12   MAXIMUM AGES OF RINGED BIRDS RECOVERED 1960–9
INCLUSIVE

Species	Total recoveries	Range of maximum ages	Mean of maximum ages
Great tit	1,466	$5\frac{6}{12}$–10 years	$7\frac{10}{12}$ years
Blue tit	3,436	$7\frac{2}{12}$–11 years	$8\frac{8}{12}$ years
Song thrush	3,670	$5\frac{9}{12}$–$10\frac{2}{12}$ years	8 years
Robin	2,009	$4\frac{8}{12}$–$6\frac{4}{12}$ years	$5\frac{7}{12}$ years
Greenfinch	5,241	$3\frac{2}{12}$–11 years	$6\frac{9}{12}$ years

Dr A. R. Jennings of the Department of Animal Pathology at Cambridge has kindly summarised the results of post-mortem examinations on 87 adult and juvenile *Parus* tits (44 blue, 39 great, 3 coal, 1 willow), and grouped the immediate causes of death as follows: infection 30, injury and predation 21, parasitic disease 10, suspected poisoning 7, organic disease 5, unknown 14. Dr Jennings emphasises the difficulty of determining the immediate cause of death of free-living wild birds, which may be heavily parasitised, malnourished and suffering from other lesions at the same time. 'Badly nourished birds are the first to die from exposure, from parasitism and from disease of any kind.' He remarks that the figure for death from infection is biased by the fact that 13 great tits and 12 blue tits died in Madingley Wood near Cambridge in 1952–3 from a virus infection of the central nervous system. The tit population of the wood had been closely studied for some years and unless very detailed post-mortem examinations had been carried out a wrong diagnosis could have been made. Although the proportion of deaths from infection may be abnormally high in this sample, mortality from outbreaks of infectious disease could easily be overlooked elsewhere.

Death from accidental injury may be frequent on roads or near houses. An analysis of the reported causes of death of ringed birds recovered in Britain over a period of five years showed that 18 per cent of the blue tits and 14 per cent of the great tits were killed by traffic.[3] The percentage for blue tits is, surprisingly, higher than that for dunnocks, bullfinches, willow warblers or house-sparrows. These figures provide an interesting comparison between species, but give little indication of the actual percentage of total tit deaths due to road injury: a dead bird on a road is conspicuous and the cause of its death evident, while a small bird corpse in a wood is rarely noticed and the cause of death usually beyond amateur diagnosis. The common tit species suffer occasional casualties from flying into windows or drowning in steep-sided garden pools or water tanks. Blue tits are often caught in mouse-traps left uncovered, carelessly or intentionally, in gardens, but deaths due to human 'control' probably have a negligible effect on the total population.

In a rural environment predation is an obvious cause of sudden death, but one that is difficult to assess in quantitative terms. It has already been mentioned in Chapter 5 that weasels may kill nestlings and brooding adult tits. J. R. Krebs found that the predation of weasels on great tit nests with eggs increased with the density of the great tit population, but there was no such increase in predation upon nestlings.[4] Thus, hatching success was found to be 'density-dependent', but not fledging success. These results refer to woods near Oxford with a generous distribution of nest-boxes, and it is probable that weasels, like woodpeckers, learn to associate boxes with food, so the destruction of clutches of tits' eggs is probably not as common, or as density-dependent, in woods where the birds are nesting in a variety of different kinds of natural holes at varying heights.

But the most effective predator upon tits in woods and many rural gardens is the sparrowhawk. L. Tinbergen estimated that 44 per cent of the mortality of great tits in certain woods in the Netherlands was due to sparrowhawks.[5] Yet the drastic reduction in the numbers of sparrowhawks in southern and midland England in the 1950s and 1960s did not appear to bring a corresponding increase among the tits. Owls also take some tits: I have found the tarsi of two blue tits with numbered rings in tawny owl pellets in my garden.

In the neighbourhood of houses and farms, the domestic or feral cat is probably the most dangerous predator for tits as for other small birds. The effects of predation are likely to be most severe in late summer and early autumn when inexperienced juvenile tits are comparatively easy victims, and when the numbers of hawks and owls, including adults, nestlings and fledged young, will be at their maximum.

Some fifty years of scientific research in the Netherlands and up to thirty years in Britain and Belgium into the problem of the natural regulation of numbers in the great tit has produced a wealth of information about its breeding biology and reproductive rates in varying conditions, and also some valuable facts and figures about mortality rates and the seasons and conditions when the heaviest losses occur, but a precise diagnosis of the most significant causes of death has still proved elusive. The discoveries made concerning the British tits must be considered in relation to David Lack's belief that 'density-dependent mortality provides the best explanation of the balance between birth and death rates' and that this mortality is chiefly due to starvation.

In Chapter 4 it was shown that the date at which tits lay their first egg is partly controlled by the availability of sufficient food for the female to produce eggs, and that the size of the clutch seems to be adapted in certain respects to the prospects of food for the nestlings three or four weeks ahead. The figures given in Chapter 5 for fledging success in different habitats confirm the importance of food supply in controlling reproductive rates. C. M. Perrins has shown convincing evidence that heavy nestlings have a much better chance of post-fledging survival than light ones.[6] Nestlings were colour-ringed in classes according to their weight at the age of 15 days, and the numbers of each colour seen in the following July were recorded (Table 13).

After the autumn leaf-fall it is easier to trap tits in woods, and as all the nestlings in the Marley boxes had been marked with numbered rings it became possible to trace in more detail the survival of juveniles in relation to parental age, brood size, nestling weight and date of hatching. As only 45 great tits out of 5,784 ringed as nestlings on the Wytham estate had been recovered outside the estate, compared with 614 recovered within it, Dr Perrins concluded that the disappearance of ringed birds indicated their death.

He has also shown that fledglings from early broods survive better than those from late ones, and in most years fewer young survive from

TABLE 13 PROPORTION OF MARKED YOUNG GREAT TITS SEEN ALIVE
JULY 1963 IN RELATION TO THEIR WEIGHT ON 15TH DAY IN NEST
(FROM PERRINS, 1965)

Nestling weight in gm, 15th day	Number fledged and ringed	Colour rings seen (July)	
		Number	percentage
Up to 15·9	39	0	0
16·0–17·9	182	5	3
18·0–18·9	269	13	5
19·0–19·9	405	33	8
20·0–20·9	268	30	11
21·0 or more	89	9	10

Note:
Many light and undernourished fledglings had thus already been eliminated by the end of June.

broods that are larger than average. Moreover, he found that in each of the years 1960–3 inclusive, nestlings with a first-year female parent did not survive as well as those with more experienced mothers. In Belgium, A. Dhondt discovered that fledglings raised during a period of warm weather had a higher survival rate than those raised in cold conditions, and he believed that yearly fluctuations in juvenile survival were mainly caused by variations in temperature when the young were in the nest.[7]

All these factors affecting the survival of young great tits—weight as nestling, date of hatching, brood-size, parental experience and weather during the nestling period—seem to indicate the death of the less favoured individuals from starvation, or at least from some degree of malnutrition combined with other influences. This explanation is supported by the fact that the most productive brood-size was high in years when caterpillars were abundant and great tits sparse, and low in years when caterpillars appeared to be scarce and great tits abundant.

However, H. N. Kluijver attributed the disappearance of juvenile great tits in late summer and early autumn, especially the young of late and second broods, to emigration caused by intraspecific competition, the younger and weaker birds being driven out by older and stronger ones.[8] This disappearance of young was less marked when the sizes of broods were experimentally reduced, so he deduced a density-dependent control of local populations due not to food shortage but to conflict between individual birds.

Summer food supplies may be less abundant in English woods than in continental ones. This is suggested by the comparative rarity of great tits' second broods in England, where there is little indication of movements of juveniles comparable to those found in Belgium and the Netherlands. Nevertheless, if summer is normally a period of food shortage for tits in Britain it is curious that it is also the season when they chiefly indulge in leisure occupations like sunbathing and prolonged preening and when they go to roost an hour or so before sunset. Perhaps it is the inexperience of newly independent juveniles both in recognising and collecting food and in evading predators and other dangers that is responsible for much of their mortality rather than an absolute shortage of food, at least in an average year. More information is still needed about the kinds and quantity of food available for young tits after fledging and their ability to exploit the resources of various habitats.

The Oxford studies have shown that the year-to-year variations in the survival of juveniles for the first few weeks after fledging play the major part in determining the numbers of great and blue tits breeding in the following season. Regular trapping through the late autumn and winter made it possible to calculate the proportion of first-winter birds to fully adult ones. The differences in the ratio of juveniles to adults are striking. They are shown in Table 14 which summarises certain features of changes in great tit populations in Marley Wood near Oxford over a period of 17 years (this is continued overleaf, with explanatory notes).

TABLE 14   POPULATION CHANGES OF THE GREAT TIT IN
MARLEY WOOD[9]

Year (i)	No of breeding ads (ii)	No of young flying Total (iii)	Per pair (iv)	% loss summer– spring (v)	Juv : adult ratio winter (vi)	Beech- mast (vii)	Winter cold (viii)
1950	62	190	6·1	75		8	10
1951	64	157	4·9	82	0·3	0	6
1952	40	150	7·5	78		3	16
1953	42	184	8·8	73	1·3	5	35
1954	62	262	8·5	83	0·5	0	25

Year (i)	No of breeding ads (ii)	No of young flying Total (iii)	No of young flying Per pair (iv)	% loss summer– spring (v)	Juv : adult ratio winter (vi)	Beech- mast (vii)	Winter cold (viii)
1955	54	183	6·8	80		0	58
1956	48	189	7·9	59		6	5
1957	98	225	4·6	83	0·2	0	14
1958	54	150	5·6	60	1·5	4	14
1959	82	277	6·8	72	1·0	0	6
1960	102	274	5·4	53	2·0	5	1
1961	172	365	4·2	83	0·2	0	47
1962	86	226	5·3	72	2·6–0·4	4	165
1963	78	253	6·5	67	1·0	0	15
1964	108						

Notes:

(a) The juvenile : adult ratio at the time of fledging will be half the figure given in column (iv) for the number flying per pair, for example 3·4:1 in 1959, 2·7:1 in 1960.

(b) Column (v) shows the difference between the total of adults plus young at the end of the breeding season and the number of breeding adults the following summer as a percentage of the former total.

(c) Column (vi) shows the proportion of first-winter to older birds in the great tits trapped during the winter.

(d) Column (vii) rates the beech-mast crop each year on an arbitrary scale in which 0 represents crop failure, 4 a moderate crop and 8 an abundant one.

(e) Column (viii) gives the sum of degrees Centigrade below freezing point for all days in each winter at Oxford on which the average temperature was below zero. (Note that the figure for the winter of 1962–3 is given on the line beginning 1962; similarly for other winters.)

When the production rate of fledged young was exceptionally low, as in 1951, 1957 and 1961, the juvenile to adult ratio was also low in the following winter, but other summers with low production rates, for instance 1958 and 1960, were followed by winters with high juvenile to adult ratios. This shows that in most years the chief factor affecting the winter ratio is not the number of young fledged but the loss of juveniles between fledging and autumn. A high ratio in winter was almost invariably followed by an increase in the number of breeding pairs in the following summer, and a low ratio by a decrease.

Table 14 does not suggest that the numbers of great tits breeding in one year influence any change of population the following year. For example the high numbers in 1960 were followed by much higher ones in 1961, and there were successive decreases from 1954 to 1956. There is no evidence in this table that juvenile mortality between summer and winter has been significantly affected by population density.

The grading of beech-mast crops in column (vii) refers to Oxford, but in fact fluctuations in this crop, and also in great tit populations, were generally found to vary in parallel in other parts of Britain and in the Netherlands. Beeches have a strong tendency towards alternate-year cropping, but unfavourable spring weather either in the same or the preceding year may cause a light crop or none when a heavy one would be due. As already seen, beech-mast is a favourite food for great, blue, coal and marsh tits, so it would not be surprising to find that the size of the crop affected the survival of these species in late autumn and winter. Indeed the table shows an increase in the breeding population of great tits after most autumns with a good crop of beech-mast and a decrease when there had been little or none. But the strongest correlation is between the mast crop and the ratio of juveniles to adults in winter. Of the 13 winters in which this ratio was measured, the four with the lowest ratio were seasons with no beech-mast, and the four with the highest ratio had a heavy or moderate crop. Yet the survival of juveniles appears to be mainly decided in the first few weeks after they leave the nest, and beech-mast does not fall and become available for great tits until about the end of October. Moreover, Kluijver found that great tits on Vlieland, one of the Friesian Islands, fluctuated in parallel with those in Marley and other woods in England and Holland although there are no beeches on the island. It has been suggested, but not proved, that a good beech-mast crop in October may be an indicator of a general abundance of food in late summer.

The last column of Table 14 puts a numerical value on the degree of coldness of winters in Oxford. It gives little support to the popular belief that great and blue tits suffer heavy losses in cold winters. Even after the most severe winter of the century, in 1962–3, the breeding population of great tits in Marley Wood had only decreased by 9 per cent from the previous year, and blue tits had actually increased from 21 pairs to 41. The other winters show little or no correlation between low temperatures and great tit mortality: two of the winters with the heaviest percentage losses were mild ones. However, H. N. Kluijver found a reduction in great tit populations in Dutch woods after some

Life and Death

cold winters, especially when previous numbers were high. The effect
of heavy rain upon food supplies and the survival of juveniles also
deserves consideration.

Although it is the losses of juveniles between summer and winter
that seem to have the most decisive effect on breeding populations in
the following spring, there is considerable mortality of adult great tits
at all seasons, varying from one year to another. C. M. Perrins caught
the breeding females in Marley Wood from 1961 to 1964 inclusive and
compared the numbers of yearling and older birds in successive years.
The losses of adult females from one spring to the next for these four
years were 39, 60, 36 and 16 per cent. The mortality of adults does not
show any correlation with existing population density.

When Dr Kluijver experimentally reduced great tit clutches on the
island of Vlieland to about 40 per cent of the normal size this resulted
in the doubling of the annual survival rate of the adults.[10] Abnormally
small clutches should reduce territorial rivalry and competition for food,
but one would expect these results to affect juveniles more than adults.
The effect upon adults might suggest that in normal circumstances
some of them die as a result of exhaustion after raising their broods.

The figures for blue tits in Marley Wood are less complete than
those for great tits, but the year-to-year changes in juvenile to adult
ratio in winter, and in breeding population generally, ran parallel with
those of great tits. They show no correlation with the production of
young in the preceding summer.

The numbers of the coal tits studied by J. A. Gibb in Breckland pine
plantations did not vary in the same way as those of great tits in broad-
leaved woods. Both species have reduced clutches of eggs when the
population density is high, and in both species variations in reproductive
success had little effect on the numbers of breeding pairs in the following summer, but there the resemblance ends. In each autumn of the
four years of the study, about half the coal tits disappeared from the
study area. Dr Gibb believed that, as food was abundant in the pines
from July to September, the late summer drop in numbers must be due
to emigration from the area, probably caused by territorial conflicts.
As this loss only varied from 47 to 54 per cent in the four years, it
could not account for the large year-to-year population changes. The
main factor regulating the numbers of breeding pairs in spring was

192

the disappearance, believed to be due to mortality, of coal tits during the winter. This loss varied greatly from one year to another, and there was convincing evidence that it was related to the quantity of food in the pines. The abundance of animal food was affected by winter temperatures, as aphids in particular continue to reproduce in a mild winter. This is well shown in the figures for 1956–7 in Table 15.[11]

It was shown in Chapter 10 that in some winters blue and coal tits removed over half the total stock of certain insect larvae from pine cones. This fact suggests that if the birds' numbers are high they may seriously deplete their food supply before spring and their winter mortality would thus be affected by their own population density.

TABLE 15   SURVIVAL OF COAL TITS IN RELATION TO INVERTEBRATE STOCKS ON PINE NEEDLES IN THE BRECKLAND (LACK, 1966 FROM GIBB'S DATA)

	1953–4	1954–5	1955–6	1956–7
Percentage of coal tits surviving, October–March	83	40	49	100
Number of coal tits present in March	77	54	58	110
Lowest level of invertebrate stock on needles, mg/m^2	111	16	72	133
Mean air temperature (° C) in January	3·3	1·4	1·9	5·2

To sum up, the evidence for starvation as the most important factor in the control of tit populations is strong but not entirely conclusive. It seems to be well established for coal tits in the artificially homogeneous habitat of pine plantations, but the evidence for similar control of great and blue tit populations in broad-leaved woods is less convincing, though perhaps only because of the practical difficulties of measuring food stocks in deciduous woodland. The data from both English and Dutch woods show that the disappearance of juveniles during the first few weeks after fledging is critical in determining the following year's breeding population, and C. M. Perrins has produced an impressive weight of fact and argument to show that this disappearance must be due to mortality through starvation. On the other hand, H. N. Kluijver's views on the improbability of food shortage in late summer and autumn may be supported by the fact that the numbers of great and blue tits in Marley Wood were not affected (like those of the Breckland coal tits) by low winter temperatures, and an increase in food supplies between autumn and winter seems unlikely.

Moreover, one would expect any starving tits to succumb in their roost-holes in the long winter nights, yet in early spring I have inspected hundreds of nest-boxes, many of which had been used for roosting, without finding a single dead bird; and this is a common experience. Although it seems likely that starvation exerts a controlling influence on the populations of all species of tits at certain times, the actual operation of this control is difficult to observe. At least as far as the great tit is concerned, it is equally difficult to prove that survival or death is affected by density of population once the young have left the nest. There is good evidence of density-dependent control of the reproductive rate but not of the mortality rate. However, Dr Lack observes that the absence of conclusive evidence of density-dependent regulation of numbers does not prove that it is not in operation: it may simply be obscured by more obvious factors such as weather changes.

On the other hand it is difficult to see how density-dependent regulation of numbers can operate upon the scarcer tit species. Intraspecific competition can hardly affect the numbers of crested tits in Scottish pine forests, of willow tits in most English woodlands or of marsh tits in some Welsh ones. In each case a pair or an individual may be miles from its nearest neighbour, and yet the numbers of the scarce species remain as stable as those of the common ones. If the principle of 'ecological isolation' discussed in Chapter 7 has any validity, this stability can hardly be attributed to competition from other species. The rarer species apparently have more specialised requirements than the common ones in respect of habitat, food and nest-sites, but it is still not obvious why they remain so thinly distributed in areas where their needs appear to be adequately met.

FUTURE OUTLOOK

In the light of present knowledge of the requirements of the different tit species, it is possible to attempt a forecast of their future prospects. For our rarest species, the crested tit, the outlook is encouraging. As long as the remains of the old Caledonian Forest are kept in their present semi-natural condition the population should be maintained, and as recent plantings of pine and spruce mature the crested tits may colonise them in increasing numbers, especially if nest-boxes can be devised to suit their tastes. Future trends for the willow tit are more difficult to predict, because the reasons for the contraction of its range in Scotland during the present century are not understood and it is not certain that the process has now ended. Within the willow tit's geographical range in Britain the conservation of damp birch and willow woods with plenty of standing dead trunks would be a useful practical step towards safeguarding the future of a local and interesting species.

The fortunes of marsh and coal tits are bound up with future forestry policy. It would be absurd to suggest that the survival of the attractive little marsh tit is at present seriously threatened, but the virtual disappearance of 'coppice with standards' and the tendency to replace broad-leaved woodland by plantations of conifers must inevitably affect its distribution and numbers. The marsh tit's loss should be the coal tit's gain, and the great new forests of spruce in hill country and pine in the lowlands must have greatly increased the numbers of coal tits in Britain. However, foresters now prefer Corsican pine to Scots because, besides growing faster, it is comparatively free from insect pests. Consequently it provides less food for tits, as was clearly shown in the Breckland studies; and any such change from native to exotic tree species is a disadvantage for insectivorous birds.

Great and blue tits are so abundant in such a wide variety of habitats, and are so generously supplied with bird-food and nest-boxes, that it may seem perversely pessimistic to point out certain trends that are unfavourable for both species. One of these is the change from broad-leaved woodland to conifer plantation, which must affect these two birds as well as the marsh tit, though less drastically. Another is the felling of big hedgerow trees, either as a result of deliberate hedge-clearance or of elm disease, and the third is the replacement of large well-timbered gardens, relics of a period of cheap labour, by housing estates with only an occasional flowering shrub. This decrease in the number of well-grown broad-leaved trees must be unfavourable for breeding great and blue tits, especially in the critical period after the fledging of the young.

Fortunately there are signs that these trends may be modified as people become aware of their implications, and it is unlikely that we shall see them carried to their logical extreme with the British blue tit spending the summer breeding in woodland nature reserves and the winter eating peanuts in small gardens. The common titmice, like several of the warblers, can flourish without extensive woodlands, but if they are to continue to delight us in anything like their present numbers we must find room, somewhere in our complex of urban development, agricultural modernisation and commercial forestry, for a generous scattering of varied indigenous trees. And, incidentally, a favourable habitat for blue tits might provide a more attractive environment for men.

Bibliographical Notes
and References

———◆———

CHAPTER TWO   The British Tits
For succinct guidance on the identification and distribution of European tits, see *A Field Guide to the Birds of Britain and Europe* by Peterson, Mountfort and Hollom, or *The Birds of Britain and Europe* by Heinzel, Fitter and Parslow. For details of structure, plumage and behaviour, *The Handbook of British Birds* by Witherby, Jourdain, Ticehurst and Tucker is still a mine of information.

1 Gompertz, T. 1961. The vocabulary of the great tit. *Brit Birds*, 54:369–94, 409–18.

CHAPTER THREE   The Preliminaries of the Breeding Cycle
1 Yapp, W. B. 1962. *Birds and Woods* (Oxford).
   Simms, E. 1971. *Woodland Birds*.
2 Deadman, A. J. 1973. The coal tit. *Forestry Commission Forest Record*, 85.
3 Gibb, J. A. and Betts, M. M. 1963. Food and food supply of nestling tits (*Paridae*) in Breckland pine. *J Anim Ecol*, 32:489–533.
4 Snow, D. W. 1954. The habitats of Eurasian tits (*Parus* spp). *Ibis*, 96: 565–85.
5 Lack, D. 1971. *Ecological isolation in birds* (Oxford).
6 Deadman, A. J. *in litt.*
7 Foster, J. and Godfrey, C. 1950. A study of the British willow tit. *Brit Birds*, 43:351–61.
8 Gibb, J. 1960. Populations of tits and goldcrests and their food supply in pine plantations. *Ibis*, 102:163–208.
9 Hinde, R. A. 1952. The behaviour of the great tit *Parus major* and some other related species. *Behaviour*, Supplement 2.
10 Haartmann, L. von. 1956. Territory in the pied flycatcher *Muscicapa hypoleuca*. *Ibis*, 98:460–75.

11 Campbell, B. 1971. The crested tit (revised edn). *Forestry Commission Leaflet*, 41.
12 Gompertz, T. 1961. The vocabulary of the great tit. *Brit Birds*, 54:369–94; 409–18.
    ——. 1971. Sounds for survival. *Birds*, 3:176–82.
13 Crooke, M. 1965. Studies on tit and pine looper populations at Culbin Forest, Morayshire. *Rep For Res*, 1965:190–200.
14 Smith, S. 1940. Some notes on the Scottish crested tit. *Brit Birds*, 34:166–71.
15 Lack, D. and E. 1958. The nesting of the long-tailed tit. *Bird Study*, 5:1–19.
16 Gibb, J. 1956. Territory in the genus *Parus*. *Ibis*, 98:420–9.
17 Kluijver, H. N. and Tinbergen, L. 1953. Territory and the regulation of density in titmice. *Arch néerl zool*, 10:265–89.
18 Krebs, J. R. 1971. Territory and feeding density in the great tit *Parus major* L. *Ecology*, 52:2–22.
19 Campbell, B. 1968. The Dean nest-box study 1942–64. *Forestry*, 41:27–46.
20 Lack, D. 1966. *Population Studies of Birds* (Oxford).
21 Morley, A. 1953. Field observations on the biology of the marsh tit. *Brit Birds*, 46:233–8, 273–87, 332–46.
22 Tooby, J. 1948. Notes on the behaviour of blue and long-tailed tits in winter flocks. *Brit Birds*, 41:258–60.
23 Stokes, A. W. 1960. Nest-site selection and courtship behaviour of the blue tit *Parus caeruleus*. *Ibis*, 102:507–18.
24 Teagle, W. G. 1948. Display of coal tit. *Brit Birds*, 41:307–8.
25 Nethersole-Thompson, D. in Witherby's *Handbook of British Birds*.

CHAPTER FOUR The Nest and Eggs
 1 Nest Record Cards are issued by the British Trust for Ornithology and completed cards are filed at the Trust's headquarters at Beech Grove, Tring, Hertfordshire.
 2 May, H. D. 1972. The birds of Botany Bay Wood, south-east Lancashire. *Nature in Lancashire*, 3:46–56.
 3 Tichy, in Crooke, M. 1965. Studies on tit and pine looper populations at Culbin Forest, Morayshire. *Rep For Res*, 1965:190–200.
 4 Campbell, B. 1968. The Dean nest-box study 1942–1964. *Forestry*, 41:27–46.
 5 Ridpath, M. G. 1951. Blue tit excavating nest-hole. *Brit Birds*, 44:278–9.
 6 Ross, W. M. 1935. Excavation of nest-hole and incubation of crested tit. *Brit Birds*, 28:226–9.
 7 Gibb, J. 1950. The breeding biology of the great and blue titmice. *Ibis*, 92:507–34.
 8 Lack, D. and E. 1958. The nesting of the long-tailed tit. *Bird Study*, 5:1–19.
 9 Miss B. Walker *in litt*.
10 Widgery, J. P. *in litt* to B. Campbell.

11 Frost, R. A. and Walker, R. B. 1973. Long-tailed tits using polystyrene as nesting material. *Brit Birds*, 66:496-7.

12 Royama, T. 1966. A re-interpretation of courtship feeding. *Bird Study*, 13:116-29.

13 Deadman, A. J. *in litt.*

14 Perrins, C. M. 1965. Population fluctuations and clutch-size in the great tit *Parus major* L. *J Anim Ecol*, 34:601-47.

——. 1970. The timing of breeding seasons. *Ibis*, 112:242-55.

15 Jones, P. J. 1972. Food as a proximate factor regulating the breeding season of the great tit *Parus major*. *Proc XVth Internat Ornith Cong*, 657-8.
Källander, H. 1974. Advancement of laying of great tits by the provision of food. *Ibis*, 116:365-7.

16 Krebs, J. R. 1970. Regulation of numbers in the great tit. *J Zool Lond*, 162:317-33.

17 Deadman, A. J. 1973. The coal tit. *Forestry Commission Forest Record*, 85.

18 Bösiger, E. and Lecomte, J. 1959. Sur les réactions des mésanges à des modifications apportées à leur nid. *Alauda*, 27:16-22.

CHAPTER FIVE The Nestlings

1 Gibb, J. 1950. The breeding biology of the great and blue titmice. *Ibis*, 92:507-39.

2 Betts, M. M. 1955. The food of titmice in oak woodland. *J Anim Ecol*, 24:282-323.

3 Gilbert, H. A. and Brook, A. 1924. *Secrets of Bird Life*.

4 Deadman, A. J. 1973. The breeding biology of the coal tit and crested tit. *Ibis*, 115:475.

5 Royama, T. 1970. Factors governing the hunting behaviour and selection of food by the great tit *Parus major* L. *J Anim Ecol*, 39:619-68.

6 Pullen, N. D. 1946. Further notes on the breeding of blue tits. *Brit Birds*, 39:162-7.

7 Arnold, G. A. and Arnold, M. A. 1952. The nesting of a pair of blue tits. *Brit Birds*, 45:175-80.

8 Gibb, J. 1955. Feeding rates of great tits. *Brit Birds*, 48:49-58.

9 Mertens, J. A. L. 1969. The influence of brood size on the energy metabolism and water loss of nestling great tits *Parus major major*. *Ibis*, 111:11-16.

10 Lawson, D. F. 1950. Blue tit feeding nestling blackbirds. *Brit Birds*, 43:186.

11 Antoine, N. J. 1959. Blue tit feeding young treecreepers. *Brit Birds*, 52:432-3.

12 Lack, D. 1958. A quantitative breeding study of British tits. *Ardea*, 46:91-124.

13 Kluijver, H. N. 1950. Daily routines of the great tit. *Ardea*, 38:99-135.

CHAPTER SIX Flocks, Local Movements and Migration

1 Kluijver, H. N. 1950. Daily routines of the great tit. *Ardea*, 38:99-135.

2 Lord, J. and Munns, D. J. 1970. *Atlas of breeding birds of the West Midlands.*
3 Gaston, A. J. 1973. The ecology and behaviour of the long-tailed tit. *Ibis*, 115:330–51.
4 Krebs, J. R., MacRoberts, M. H. and Cullen, J. M. 1972. Flocking and feeding in the great tit *Parus major*—an experimental study. *Ibis*, 114:507–30.
5 Morse, D. H. 1973. Interactions between tit flocks and sparrowhawks *Accipiter nisus*. *Ibis*, 115:591–3.
6 Goodbody, I. M. 1952. The post-fledging dispersal of juvenile titmice. *Brit Birds*, 45:279–85.
7 Perrins, C. M. 1963. Survival in the great tit, *Parus major*. *Proc Internat Orn Cong*, 13:717–28.
8 Figures obtained from the annual reports of the Ringing & Migration Committee of the British Trust for Ornithology, published in *Brit Birds*.
9 Cramp, S., Pettet, R. and Sharrock, J. T. R. 1960. The irruption of tits in autumn 1957. *Brit Birds*, 53:49–77, 99–117, 176–92.
   Cramp, S. 1963. Movements of tits in Europe in 1959 and after. *Brit Birds*, 56:237–63.
10 Lack, D. 1954. *The natural regulation of animal numbers* (Oxford).
11 Svärdson, G. 1957. The invasion type of bird migration. *Brit Birds*, 50:314–43.
12 Perrins, C. M. 1966. The effect of beech crops on great tit populations and movements. *Brit Birds*, 59:419–31.

CHAPTER SEVEN Feeding and Food-storing
1 Lack, D. 1971. *Ecological isolation in birds* (Oxford).
2 Hartley, P. H. T. 1953. An ecological study of the feeding habits of the English titmice. *J Anim Ecol*, 22:261–88.
   Gibb, J. 1954. Feeding ecology of tits, with notes on treecreeper and goldcrest. *Ibis*, 96:513–44.
3 Betts, M. M. 1955. The food of titmice in oak woodland. *J Anim Ecol*, 24:282–323.
4 Yapp, W. B. 1962. *Birds and Woods.*
5 Williamson, R. and Williamson, K. 1973. The bird community of yew woodland at Kingley Vale, Sussex. *Brit Birds*, 66:12–23.
6 Gibb, J. 1960. Populations of tits and goldcrests and their food supply in pine plantations. *Ibis*, 102:163–208.
7 Haftorn, S. 1954–6. Contribution to the food biology of tits, especially about storing of surplus food. *Det Kgl Norske Vidensk Skrifter*, 1953 no 4, 1956 no 2.
8 Saunders, H. 1899. *An illustrated manual of British birds.*
9 Caris, J. L. 1958. Great tit killing and carrying goldcrest. *Brit Birds*, 51:355.
10 Mylne, C. K. 1959. Birds drinking the sap of a birch tree. *Brit Birds*, 52:426–7.

11 Vince, M. A. 1960. Developmental changes in responsiveness in great tits. *Behav*, 15:219–43.
12 Hall-Craggs, J. 1959. Feeding methods of long-tailed tits with artificial food. *Brit Birds*, 52:21.
13 Coward, T. 1920. *Birds of the British Isles and their eggs*, vol 1.
14 Witherby, H. F., Jourdain, F. C. R., Ticehurst, N. F. and Tucker, B. W. 1938. *The Handbook of British Birds*, vol 1.
15 Owen, J. H. 1945. Unusual feeding behaviour of tits. *Brit Birds*, 38:173.
16 Hart, D. 1958. Hoarding of food by willow tit. *Brit Birds*, 51:122.

CHAPTER EIGHT Miscellaneous Activities
 1 Gibb, J. 1960. Populations of tits . . . in pine plantations. *Ibis*, 102:163–208.
 2 Williams, T. S. 1946. Sunbathing habit of juvenile great tits. *Brit Birds*, 39:152.
 3 Colyer, W. L. 1946. Sunbathing of long-tailed tit. *Brit Birds*, 39:245–6.
 4 Kennedy, R. J. 1969. Sunbathing behaviour in birds. *Brit Birds*, 62:249–58.
 5 Goodwin, D. 1967. Some possible functions of sunbathing in birds. *Brit Birds*, 60:363–4.
 6 Barnes, P. G. D. *in litt*.
 7 Muddeman, F. E. 1960. Anting by blue tits. *Brit Birds*, 50:17.
 8 Hancock, M. 1965. Birds bathing in snow and wet grass, leaves and earth. *Brit Birds*, 58:155–6.
 9 Upton, W. 1968. Bathing activity of great tit. *Brit Birds*, 61:312–13.
10 Clague, W. D. 1949. Blue tit snow-bathing. *Brit Birds*, 42:23.
11 Smith, I. 1969. Blue tit bathing in snow. *Brit Birds*, 62:202.
12 Kennedy, R. J. 1970. Direct effects of rain on birds: a review. *Brit Birds*, 63:401–14.
13 Ruttledge, R. F. 1946. Roosting habits of the Irish coal tit. *Brit Birds*, 39:326–33.
14 Dunsheath, M. H. and Doncaster, C. C. 1941. Some observations on roosting birds. *Brit Birds*, 35:138–48.
15 Errington, F. P. 1961. Blue tits roosting in streetlamps. *Brit Birds*, 54:287–8.
16 Gooch, G. B. 1938. Blue tit's swinging roost. *Brit Birds*, 31:252–3.
17 Eygenraam in Kluijver, H. N. 1951. The population ecology of the great tit, *Parus m. major* L. *Ardea*, 39:1–135.
18 May, D. J. 1947. Roosting of British coal tit. *Brit Birds*, 41:346–7.
19 Marples, G. 1935. Observations on times of feeding. *Brit Birds*, 29:43–9.

CHAPTER NINE Individuality and Intelligence
 1 Brian, A. D. 1949. Dominance in the great tit. *Scot Nat*, 61:144–55.
 2 Colquhoun, M. K. 1942. Notes on the social behaviour of blue tits. *Brit Birds*, 35:234–40.
 3 Thorpe, W. H. in Landsborough Thomson, A. 1964. *New dictionary of birds*.
 4 Buxton, E. J. M. 1948. Tits and peanuts. *Brit Birds*, 41:229–32.

5 Thorpe, W. H. 1956. *Learning and instinct in animals.*
6 Vince, M. A. 1958. String-pulling in birds: individual differences in wild adult great tits. *Brit J Anim Behav,* 4:111–16.
7 Brooks-King, M. 1941. Intelligence tests with tits. *Brit Birds,* 35:29–32.
8 Brooks-King, M. and Hurrell, H. G. 1958. Intelligence tests with tits. *Brit Birds,* 51:514–24.
9 Thorpe, W. H. 1951. Learning abilities of birds. *Ibis,* 93:1–52.

CHAPTER TEN   Pests or Pest-controllers?
1 Yarrell, W. 1837. *A history of British birds.*
2 Macgillivray, W. 1837. *A history of British birds.*
3 Harthan, A. J. 1942. Marsh tits and wood pigeons feeding upon plum blossom. *Brit Birds,* 36:141.
4 Wright, E. N. 1959. Bird damage to horticultural crops. *J Roy Hort Soc,* 84:426–34.
5 Wright, E. N. and Brough, T. 1966. Bird damage to fruit, present and future. *Roy Hort Soc,* 1966:168–80.
6 Murton, R. K. 1971. *Man and birds.*
7 Manley, R. O. B. 1948. *Bee-keeping in Britain.*
8 Almond, W. E. 1959. Great tit stung to death by bees. *Brit Birds,* 52:314.
9 Betts, M. M. 1955. The food of titmice in oak woodland. *J Anim Ecol,* 24: 282–323.
10 Brian, M. V. and Brian, A. D. 1950. Bird predation of defoliating caterpillars. *Scot Nat,* 62:88–92.
11 Gibb, J. A. and Betts, M. M. 1963. Food . . . of nestling tits in Breckland pine. *J Anim Ecol,* 32:489–533.
12 Bruns, H. 1960. The economic importance of birds in forests. *Bird Study,* 7:193–208.
13 Gibb, J. 1958. Predation by tits and squirrels on the eucosmid *Ernarmonia conicolana. J Anim Ecol,* 27:375–96.
14 Gibb, J. 1960. Populations of tits . . . in pine plantations. *Ibis,* 102:163–208.
15 Smith, B. D. 1966. Effects of parasites and predators on a natural population of the aphid *Acyrthosiphon spartii* (Koch) on broom *Sarothamnus scoparius* L. *J Anim Ecol,* 35:255–67.

CHAPTER ELEVEN   Domestic Nuisances
1 Logan-Home, W. M. 1953. Paper-tearing by birds. *Brit Birds,* 46:16–21.
2 Cramp, S., Pettet, A. and Sharrock, J. T. R. 1960. The irruption of tits in autumn 1957. *Brit Birds,* 53:49–77, 99–117, 176–92.
3 Watterson, E. L. personal communication.
4 Lack, D. 1958. A quantitative breeding study of British tits. *Ardea,* 46: 91–124.
5 Hinde, R. A. 1953. A possible explanation of paper-tearing behaviour in birds. *Brit Birds,* 46:21–3.

6 Fisher, J. and Hinde, R. A. 1949. The opening of milk bottles by birds. *Brit Birds*, 42:347–57.
7 —— —— 1951. Further observations on the opening of milk bottles by birds. *Brit Birds*, 44:393–6.
8 Garrad, L. S. *in litt.*

CHAPTER TWELVE Welcome Guests
1 Allen, D. E. 1969. An overlooked pioneer. *Birds*, 2:296–7.
2 Stokes, A. W. 1962. Agonistic behaviour among blue tits at a feeding station. *Behav*, 19:118–38.
3 Perrins, C. M. 1968. The great tit and the blue tit. *Birds*, 2:32–3.
4 Kenrick, H. 1940. A study of blue tits by colour ringing. *Brit Birds*, 33: 307–10.
5 Howard, L. 1952. *Birds as individuals.*
6 Thorpe, W. H. 1944. Further notes on a type of insight learning by birds. *Brit Birds*, 38:46–9.
7 Yapp, W. B. 1970. *The life and organisation of birds.*
8 Duncan, C. J. in Landsborough Thomson, A. 1964. *A new dictionary of birds.*
9 Warren, R. P. and Vince, M. A. 1963. Taste discrimination in the great tit *Parus major. J comp physiol Psychol*, 56:91–3.
10 Newton, A. 1873 in 4th edition of Yarrell's *History of British birds.*

CHAPTER THIRTEEN Life and Death
1 Snow, D. W. 1956. The annual mortality of the blue tit in different parts of its range. *Brit Birds*, 49:174–7.
2 Kluijver, H. N. 1951. The population ecology of the great tit. *Ardea*, 39:1–135.
3 Mead, C. J. 1972. A matter of life and death. *BTO News*, 53:1–2.
4 Krebs, J. R. 1970. Regulation of numbers in the great tit. *J Zool Lond*, 162:317–33.
5 Tinbergen, L. 1946. De sperwer als rooferjand van zangvogels. *Ardea*, 34: 1–213.
6 Perrins, C. M. 1965. Population fluctuations and clutch-size in the great tit *Parus major. J Anim Ecol*, 34:601–47.
7 Dhondt, A. A. 1971. The regulation of numbers in Belgian populations of great tits. *Proc Adv Study Inst Dynamics Numbers Popul* (Oosterbeek, 1970,) 532–47.
8 Kluijver, H. N. 1972. An experimental study of the survival of young great tits. *Proc XVth Internat Orn Cong*, 661.
9 Lack, D. 1966. *Population studies of birds* (Oxford).
10 Kluijver, H. N. 1971. Regulation of numbers in populations of great tits *Parus m. major. Proc Adv Study Inst Dynamics Numbers Popul* (Oosterbeek, 1970), 507–23.
11 Table from D. Lack's *Population studies of birds*, based on data by J. Gibb.

Acknowledgements

So many people have helped me in the preparation of this book by their correspondence, their conversation or their publications, that it is impossible to mention all of them by name. However, I should like to acknowledge with especial gratitude my indebtedness to Dr Bruce Campbell for reading through and commenting upon a draft of the text and for making many valuable suggestions. The bibliographical notes to the chapters will indicate the chief published sources of information, but I have found especially helpful the books of the late Dr David Lack and articles published in scientific periodicals by his colleagues, notably Professor R. A. Hinde, Dr J. A. Gibb, Dr M. M. Betts and Dr C. M. Perrins. The pioneer study of the great tit in the Netherlands by Dr H. N. Kluijver has also been most useful. On particular species the Forestry Commission booklets on the crested tit by Bruce Campbell and the coal tit by Andrew Deadman, and the papers in *British Birds* on the marsh tit by the late Averil Morley have provided valuable information. Very different in style and content but also, I believe, a useful and stimulating source of fact and opinion are the two books on house-tamed birds by the late Miss Len Howard.

I should like to record my gratitude to the librarian and staff of the Kendal & Westmorland County Library for obtaining for me so promptly and efficiently particular issues of scientific periodicals or photocopies of articles contained in them, and to the director and librarian of the NERC Research Station at Grange-over-Sands for reading facilities there.

My own studies have been greatly assisted by the financing of a nest-box scheme by the Cumbria (formerly Lake District) Naturalists' Trust, and by the data obtained from the boxes by some members of the Trust. Similar information has been provided by members of the Lancaster & District Birdwatching Society, especially Mr J. C. Mockett.

For the drawings and figures illustrating the text I am most grateful to Jack Marshall (Fig 1) and Suzanne Barnes (Figs 2–5), and I am indebted to the authors named in the text or notes and to the publishers of certain books and periodicals for permission to reproduce certain figures and tables. Photographs are a most valuable part of a book of this kind and I am greatly obliged to Eric Hosking (Plates, pages 33, 34, 51, 102, 120), Brian and Sheila Bottomley (Plates, pages 51, 52, 101, 102), J. Allan Cash Ltd, acting for the late John Markham (Plates, pages 119, 120) and John Clegg (Plate, page 52) for the use of their excellent pictures.

Finally, I would like to thank Mrs Margaret Wilson for help with typing; and my daughter, Helen Caldwell, for proof-reading and useful comments.

Index

References to plates are in *italics*.

References to geographical locations in connection with distribution of species (pages 21–32) are omitted. Only selected topics are indexed under each tit species.